Praise for
SMALL ACTS OF LEADERSHIP
and G. SHAWN HUNTER

"Engrossing and compelling. Shawn shows how anyone can step up and quietly take the lead with small, intentional acts each day."
—Susan Cain, co-founder of Quiet Revolution and
New York Times best-selling author of *QUIET*

"*Small Acts of Leadership* pops with brave energy and honesty. This is a big, audacious book; Shawn distills the best of leadership wisdom with the most recent science in human behavior to show that anyone can take small steps every day to great leadership. One of the best business reads of the year. A triumph!"
—Marshall Goldsmith, award-winning executive coach,
New York Times and *Wall Street Journal*
best-selling author of *Triggers*

"Hunter has done the nearly impossible—he has created a business book that is simultaneously wise, insightful, and incredibly enjoyable to read. Buy it now, read it, and reap the rewards."
—Hap Klopp, founder of The North Face and
best-selling author of *ALMOST*

"*Small Acts of Leadership* is a terrific and enjoyable read. It dispels the notion that great leadership is something bestowed upon people at birth. This book demonstrates that grit and perseverance, combined with a willingness to learn, are keys to taking one's leadership to another level. Reading this book and applying its principles will make you a better leader; reading it twice might just make you a transformational leader!"
—Tom DiDonato, senior vice president,
Human Resources, Lear Corporation

"Every day we are confronted by complexity and urgency which leave us feeling we have no control over our own lives. Shawn Hunter's new book shows us that a few simple actions will help us take control and reach our full potential. Clarity, simplicity, and real-world examples of success provide a high-impact solution to the challenges of the modern world of work."

—Chris Roebuck, visiting professor of Transformational Leadership, Cass Business School, London

"This is Shawn Hunter at his very best. All grit and courage…telling stories that hit home, ring true, and point the way to a better you. This is a must-have toolbox for every manager."

—John Ambrose, general manager, SumTotal (a Skillsoft Company)

"What if you had a trusted mentor and friend who was there to guide and support you on your leadership path? That's what Shawn Hunter provides in *Small Acts of Leadership*. A gifted observer and storyteller, Shawn shares how small, mindful acts and clear intention can make the difference for you not just as a leader, but as a person."

—Scott Eblin, author of *The Next Level: What Insiders Know About Executive Success* and *Overworked and Overwhelmed: The Mindfulness Alternative*

"Shawn Hunter delivers a wealth of knowledge in *Small Acts of Leadership*. Key points from the business and psychology literatures are expertly distilled into a concise, thoughtful, and engaging narrative, allowing current or aspirational business leaders to read about critical new findings from research. Shawn also draws upon his vast experience of working with business leaders to provide relevant and entertaining examples to show how new learning from the book can be applied in real business situations. As a business school professor, I teach executives all over the world. I will definitely recommend that they read *Small Acts of Leadership*."

—Jill Klein, PhD, professor of Marketing, Melbourne Business School

SMALL ACTS
OF
LEADERSHIP

SMALL ACTS OF LEADERSHIP

12 Intentional Behaviors That Lead to Big Impact

G. SHAWN HUNTER

First published by Bibliomotion, Inc.
39 Harvard Street
Brookline, MA 02445
Tel: 617-934-2427
www.bibliomotion.com

Printed in the United States of America

Print ISBN 978-1-62956-136-3
E-book ISBN 978-1-62956-137-0
Enhanced E-book ISBN 978-1-62956-138-7

CIP data has been applied for.

For Charlie, Will, and Annie. Thank you for making Mom and me laugh and learn each day. And remember, those small, positive acts of yours create joy and purpose in the world.
Love, Dad.

Contents

INTRODUCTION

Small Things Can Matter Most

As one of the most revered coaches in American history, John Wooden, the "Wizard of Westwood," coached his UCLA Bruins basketball team to an unprecedented, and never-again-repeated, ten national championship titles in twelve years. This remarkable winning streak included an astonishing run of eighty-eight undefeated games in a row, and back-to-back 30–0 seasons.

If you had been lucky enough to get into UCLA and play basketball for the great John Wooden in the 1960s and early 1970s, you would have been surprised on your first day of practice. Instead of the opportunity to show your passing, shooting, and dribbling skills in front of the esteemed coach, your first lesson at your first practice would have been to learn to put on your socks, and lace and tie your shoes, properly.

Describing the first practice of every season, Wooden said in an interview that he would ask his players to take off their shoes and socks. Explaining that these were the most important pieces of equipment each player possessed on the court, Wooden taught his players how to carefully pull on each sock, making sure there were no wrinkles, particularly around the heel and toes, which might cause a blister.[1]

Then, advising each player to hold his socks up firmly while lacing his shoes, he told the player to pull the laces securely from each eyelet, not simply yank the laces from the top. And always, *always*, double-knot the laces, Wooden said, having no tolerance for shoes that became untied during a practice or a game. Ever.

Wooden explained that, after each player spent a few minutes following his careful instructions, he would inspect the player's work, and probably tell him that his shoes were too big, anyway, and instruct the player to show up at the next practice with shoes at least a half size smaller. Over the years, he had noticed that his players had the habit of buying shoes that were too big so the players could "grow into them," just as they had been taught as kids.[2] As a result, his players were often wearing shoes that were too big, allowing their feet to slide around during the constant stopping and starting as they ran around the court.

This is how the greatest basketball coach of all time started his first practice of each season.

This book isn't about how to put on your shoes and socks, but it is about doing little things that can lead to big impact. Small, consistent efforts, practiced over time, can yield big results for you, and the people around you.

The reason New Year's resolutions fail is not because the goal is too great or the intention is misguided. It's because the discrepancy between where we are today and the envisioned future often appears so great that we cannot bridge the gap. If we resolve to spend five days a week at the gym, and we currently spend zero, then the gap is so great that we cannot immediately and easily cross it.

This book is about small steps and tiny tweaks in how we treat ourselves, how we carry ourselves, and how we think about other people, and the world, that can change the way we think and behave.

CHAPTER 1

Believe in Yourself

The respect and regard we have for ourselves is our self-esteem. The strength of our belief in our abilities to accomplish our goals and achieve our potential is our self-efficacy.[1] These are two different things, and without self-efficacy, we are likely to fail in leading others. When we have a strong sense of self-efficacy, we take deeper interest in and make a greater commitment to our activities, we view challenges to be mastered, and we recover quickly from setbacks and pitfalls.

It's easy to think we don't know what we're doing, that those around us have a better handle on the situation and are more competent. But often that's not the case—often everyone is in the same boat, looking for a captain. By believing in ourselves, we can become that leader.

And, surprisingly, it's not always the fear of failure that keeps us from acting but rather the fear of success. We ask ourselves, if we succeed, will others have higher expectations that we can't fulfill? Will we be able to top our last success? Are we charlatans who just had some blind luck? When life comes at us hard, do we panic or do we thrive?

When life is hard, even scary, and options seem slim, letting go and embracing optimism can actually save us, put us on the right track. By avoiding panic and giving our minds some space to work, it's amazing what we can accomplish, how we can come to our own rescue.

In this chapter, we look at the traits of those who believed in themselves and survived tremendous, life-threatening challenges. Although most of us don't face such challenges on a daily basis, we do deal with stress, often extreme stress, in the workplace. We could just quit, and many people do, but wouldn't it be better to find a way to deal with the stress and, like an alchemist, turn that negative stress into positive pressure and have confidence in ourselves?

And while we often think we're lucky or unlucky, we can choose to make our own luck by facing challenges head-on, trusting our own intuition, and expecting the best outcomes. And when we believe in ourselves, we find it easier to be true to our values and live authentically instead of trying to be who we think others want us to be.

Believing We Are Impostors

Have you ever believed that you are not deserving or are worried that people will reveal you as a fraud? Have you ever thought someone else could do your job better, or thought you got that bonus or promotion by luck? Have you ever been in a hurry to leave before someone finds out you don't know what the hell you're talking about?

The feeling that we are frauds when we succeed is known as "impostor syndrome." It can be defined, according to the Caltech Counseling Center, as "a collection of feelings of inadequacy that persist even in face of information that indicates that the opposite is true. It is experienced internally as chronic self-doubt, and feelings of intellectual fraudulence."[2]

It's hard for any one to have self-confidence when she thinks she's the only one who doesn't know what she's doing. Each year, Olivia Fox Cabane, who teaches at Stanford, asks her incoming group of freshmen, "How many of you in here feel that you are the one mistake that the admissions committee made?" Each year, more than two-thirds of the students raise their hands.[3]

It's human nature to compare ourselves with others. In any given situation, we often look around and make comparisons. And these comparisons can make us feel inadequate. We know that the less we focus on comparisons the happier we will feel about ourselves, but we still can't help ourselves. Someone else is always smarter, prettier, funnier. "There are an awful lot of people out there who think I'm an expert," Dr. Margaret Chan, director-general of the World Health Organization, once said. "How do these people believe all this about me? I'm so much aware of all the things I don't know."[4]

The immensely talented and brilliant Maya Angelou authored eleven books in her lifetime. She once said, "Each time, I think, 'Uh-oh. They're going to find out now. I've run a game on everybody, and they're going to find me out.' "[5]

Kate Winslet won an Academy Award for her role in *Titanic*. After receiving the award, she said, "I'd wake up in the morning before going off to a shoot, and think, 'I can't do this. I'm a fraud.' "[6]

The interesting thing about impostor syndrome is that the more successful we become, the greater the likelihood we will encounter more bouts of self-doubt. The reason is that, as we enjoy greater and greater success, we encounter increasingly successful people with whom to compare ourselves. Here's the secret: they don't know what they are doing, either; they're just winging it, too.

Social media doesn't help. We all get to see the happier, more beautiful side of successful people online, instead of the moments of doubt, sleeplessness, and insecurity. Sure, they know something about something, which is what got them there in the first place. But, when under the influence of a self-doubt attack, we begin to believe those around us must be brilliant.

We should try to remember these truths, as I remind myself when I feel doubt: you do deserve to be here. It wasn't luck. It was your tenacity and hard work. Ambition is a good thing. Strive for more. It's okay to ask. And stop comparing—it's self-defeating. Instead, start by trying to be the person you would like to work for. It's kind of like trying to live up to, and become, the person your dog already thinks you are.

Escaping the Trance of Unworthiness

Maintaining belief in ourselves can be difficult in the face of failure. But sometimes, failing is less scary than succeeding. Failing is status quo, going back to the norm, maybe even further back to Slackville. We can allow ourselves to sink into a trance of unworthiness.

Failing can be especially terrifying when the stakes are high. It's a common misconception that successful entrepreneurs are filled with confidence, acumen, and bravado. Real estate mogul Barbara Corcoran lost nearly everything in her first failed marketing campaign. Bill Gates's first company, Traf-O-Data, was a complete bomb. Milton Hershey's famous company, Hershey's, was actually the fourth candy company he founded, after the first three failed. The point is that, while failure can be expected, those who persevere and succeed eventually don't let their failures define them.

Even success may not rid us of our feelings of self-doubt. Sometimes the thought of actually accomplishing our audacious dreams can bring as much dread as contemplating failure. Succeeding means change. Change, by definition, is unfamiliar and uncomfortable.

And succeeding can make us stand out, make us different from our peers. It can bring envy and jealousy from others, as well as hurt, notoriety, limelight, pressure, confusion, and the doubt that we can do it again. Success takes courage.

Some say each of us is the average of the five people we hang out with the most. Those people make up our posse, our tribe—they're our peeps. And the most uncomfortable idea in the world can be the threat of social and emotional isolation from our tribe. It's terrifying to think that actualizing our dreams might alienate those closest to us, simply because we are stepping outside of the group's comfort zone.

We will face hurdles on our way to taking on, and crushing, our own audacious challenges, and fear of social and emotional isolation is the first among them. To overcome this hurdle, we can start by helping others over it, and letting them know that they are safe in following their ambitions. We should cheer on and support our friends and colleagues when they step out and try something bold. Even if they bomb in their efforts, we need to make sure they don't fail because we made them feel like they don't deserve to succeed.

Sometimes the act of asserting ourselves in the face of competition can bring a wave of guilt. Playing someone else who is better than ourselves elevates our game, making us feel good to be pulled up a notch, but the inverse can be uncomfortable. When we are the one elevating the game, when we are the one quickening the pace, it can feel like we are dropping our pals and betraying loyalties.

We also sabotage ourselves by fearing that we may discover higher potential, which might make us feel unworthy or unqualified. To escape the trance of unworthiness, we should focus on competence, not confidence. Too often, we clench our fists and try to summon confidence on demand.

As Harvard professor Amy Cuddy demonstrates, when we make power poses and take an assertive posture, we enable our brain to release dopamine, and a burst of confidence can wash over us, providing a brief heightened state of confidence and joy.[7] However, true, profound confidence comes from deep competence. Our true potential is fulfilled through tenacity, as we pursue excellence and succeed.

Finally, we can feel pressure to constantly match or exceed our own previous best performance. There is a 10K road race I do every year. And every year I try to post a personal best. Usually I don't beat my previous performance, but I try to. Although that's getting tougher every year, I still believe it's possible. Last year I did manage to beat my personal best, which I first posted more than nine years ago. It's hard, but it can be done.

But here's the funny thing: I exceeded what I thought was my own capacity by approaching the problem differently. I used to train in volume by simply running more miles. Now I focus more on the quality of each run, approaching each effort with focus, concentration, and a plan. That plan may involve intervals of strenuous effort or intervals of hill climbing, or that plan may simply involve rest. Resting, as I focus on in chapter 12, is an important ingredient not only of effective training but of every aspect of life.

The pursuit of quality, rather than quantity, can bring about the greatest success in terms of personal achievement and happiness. And we can explore new outputs only by changing the inputs. One good strategy for fighting doubt is to get "pronoid." Pronoia is the opposite of paranoia. It is the belief that the world, and everyone around you, is conspiring for your success.

Thriving Instead of Panicking

M. Ephimia Morphew, a psychologist and founder of the Society for Human Performance in Extreme Environments, spent some time with her colleagues puzzling over why some novice scuba divers drown even though they have plenty of oxygen left in their tanks, as Laurence Gonzales relates in his book *Deep Survival: Who Lives, Who Dies, and Why*.[8] The reason, it turns out, is that, in a stressful and unfamiliar environment, people often start to hyperventilate because they feel like they can't breathe. And the instinctive response to that feeling is to remove any obstruction from their mouth. In a moment of panic, they rip the regulator off their face and suck in a deep breath of the ocean. It's similar to the reason those suffering from extreme hypothermia often take off all their clothes in a snowstorm.

Fear is an unpleasant emotion, to say the least. It can make us do what in other circumstances would seem irrational. It can even immobilize us. Fear is a natural reaction to changing, unpredictable situations, or the threat of imminent harm to ourselves or those around us.

While it may seem trite or clichéd to say, fear does exist only in our minds. It is our personal reaction to these changing circumstances and perceived threats, and we can change our reaction of fear, instead seeing such situations as merely challenges to be overcome, opportunities to grow. The following stories exemplify that believing anything is possible, even in the direst circumstances, can lead not only to success but, in some cases, can save our lives.

Moving from Fear to Resolve

On January 29, 1981, marine architect Steve Callahan woke abruptly from a dead sleep in the middle of the Atlantic Ocean on his little twenty-one-foot, self-made sloop. There had been a mighty crash. In the seconds before he could stand into action, the boat was already starting to list and fill with water.

Quickly, within a minute or two, he was able to deploy his self-inflating life raft and gather a few items as the boat sank. He leapt to the raft and discovered that a couple of small, airtight compartments within the sailboat were keeping it afloat—and likely only for a few moments longer.

He made a small joke to himself about how lucky he was, and calmly used the opportunity to swim inside the sinking boat to retrieve some valuable items—a flotation cushion, a sleeping bag, an emergency kit, food, a spear gun, a solar still, and a few other things.

Over the next seventy-six days, he drifted 1,800 miles west in that little raft. During the course of his journey—as his skin became covered in saltwater sores and sunburns, his raft was set upon by sharks, his radio failed to signal rescue, and his body deteriorated—he took time each evening to admire the beauty of the night sky.

Callahan's story, as he recounted in his book *Adrift*, likely would not have ended the same for everyone in that situation. According to Laurence Gonzales, when disaster strikes, those who don't succumb differ in that "they immediately begin to recognize, acknowledge, and even accept the reality of their situation.... They move through denial, anger, bargaining, depression, and acceptance very rapidly."[9]

One thing Callahan remembers vividly from the episode is that he was very calm, hyperaware, and focused throughout the sinking event, from first impact to minutes later, as he watched his boat slide under the waves. He can recount his every action. He can play the video in his mind of every nuance of the event.

Al Siebert, in his book *The Survivor Personality*, continues this thought: "The best survivors spend almost no time, especially in emergencies, getting upset about what has been lost, or feeling distressed about things going badly."[10] When things go badly, those who survive move away from the emotion of fear and toward a state of resolve.

Stress is a response to a trigger, which can be a challenge, a circumstance, a rapidly changing environment, or even a negative thought. But the extent to which the trigger induces distress or a positive sense of challenge is largely up to us. How we react to these triggers can be the difference between the two emotional states.

In psychologist Kelly McGonigal's research over an eight-year period, she found that those people who experience high levels of persistent stress had a 43 percent higher mortality rate. But that was only true for those people who also *believed* that stress has negative health consequences. According to McGonigal, it's possible for those who embrace stress to convert it into positive pressure. Under these circumstances, when stress is reinterpreted as constructive pressure, the negative health consequences are largely removed.[11]

Pressure can yield excellence. The difference between those who become paralyzed and succumb to fear and stress, and those who interpret obstacles as something to overcome, is *resolve*. Resolve is a mindset.

Seeing a Light in the Void

In 1985, Joe Simpson and his climbing partner, Simon Yates, decided to climb the massive mountain Siula Grande, in the Peruvian Andes. They didn't take the conventional route but instead chose to ascend the never-before-attempted west face of the mountain, which is nearly vertical and covered in nothing but "a sheer layer of ice, loose dirt, flat rock, motorcycle grease, melted butter and used cooking oil," as writer Ben Thompson describes it.[12]

Simpson and Yates triumph in the climb, but on the descent Simpson suffers a broken leg. Yates lowers him by rope down the mountain for hours, and then, in a rising blizzard, mistakenly lowers him over a cliff into a fathomless crevasse. After an hour, Yates cannot hold the rope any longer and believes his partner is irretrievable. It is impossible for Yates to physically pull Simpson back up to safety. In a moment of personal torment, Yates chooses to save his own life, cuts the rope, and allows Simpson to fall to his death. Miraculously, Simpson doesn't die. He awakens to find himself on his back, having survived the fifty-foot fall with a crushed knee and destroyed leg. He crawls, limps, and drags himself for three days back to camp.

Simpson recounts this story in his book *Touching the Void*, describing the ordeal of hanging on the rope for an hour, in the void, as night was turning to dawn: "A pillar of gold light beamed diagonally from a small hole in the roof. . . . I was mesmerized by this beam of sunlight burning through the vaulted ceiling from the real world outside. . . . I was going to reach that sunbeam. I knew it then with absolute certainty."[13]

Turning Workplace Stress into Opportunity

While it may seem extreme to compare the harrowing experiences described above to today's workplace, our work environment can sometimes make us feel as if we are drowning, too—or hanging onto our jobs by a rope, dangling over an abyss. A March 2015 survey of 160,000 employees around the world found that 75 percent of today's workers experience "moderate" to "extreme" stress.[14] An April 2014 survey of more than 7,000 employees by the job-hunting website Monster found that 42 percent even left their jobs because the workplace was too stressful.[15]

In the electrifying August 16, 2015, *New York Times* article, "Inside Amazon: Wrestling Big Ideas in a Bruising Workplace"—which was later rebutted, and whose validity is still deeply debated—Jodi Kantor and David Streitfeld wrote about marketer Bo Olson's take on those who succumbed to workplace stress at Amazon: "Bo Olson…lasted less than two years in a book marketing role and said that his enduring image was watching people weep in the office, a sight other workers described as well…. 'Nearly every person I worked with, I saw cry at their desk.'"[16]

In a typical stress response, heart rate and breathing increase, and blood vessels constrict. But those people who rise to challenges with the belief that stress is a positive opportunity have an opposite physiological response: the blood vessels open and relax as if they were in a state of elation or preparation for physical test.

Or, to put it in Kelly McGonigal's language, embracing adversity and challenge with a positive mindset is another way of saying that you trust yourself. It's another gesture of confidence. And that confidence and resolve will make you much more resilient for whatever challenges arise.

To take this one step further, not only can we convert negative stress into positive pressure and adopt a mindset of resolve, but we can also make ourselves luckier. Seriously.

Making Luck a Choice

Rabbit's feet, four-leaf clovers, and rain during sunshine are all thought to be signs of fortune and good luck in some cultures. The good-luck ritual of "knocking on wood" comes from pre-Christian customs in which it was considered important to invoke the powerful and benign influence of the tree gods.

Cats throughout history have been believed to be both powerful and good (ancient Egypt), and powerful and bad (medieval

England). In the 1560s, in Lincolnshire England, the story goes that a father and son chased a black cat into an alley, and then threw stones at it before it escaped to the home of a nearby woman suspected of being a witch. The next day they returned to discover the woman limping with bruised legs, presumably from the stoning the night before. That led to the belief that witches could transform into black cats.

In the same vein, when a ladder is propped up against a wall, a natural triangle is formed, symbolic of the holy Trinity. To walk under the ladder would break the Trinity, and therefore bring ill fortune. Numerous experiments demonstrate such superstitions have no real worldly effect.

In his book *The Luck Factor: The Four Essential Principles*, Richard Wiseman describes luck in terms of choice.[17] In his research working with more than four hundred individuals on something he called "The Luck Project," Wiseman found several key attributes of those who describe themselves as "lucky":

• **They create chance.** Wiseman has a fun game in which participants write down six activities or experiences they have not tried but would be willing to try, then roll a die and do the activity that corresponds to the outcome. This game reinforces our willingness to try something new, to be curious and creative.

• **They think lucky.** Decision making driven by intuition seems impossible to control, yet Wiseman discovered those lucky decision makers actually spent more time reflecting and meditating on the decision once considered, and spent more time envisioning hypothetical circumstances in which they may have to make decisions, than the other subjects. So when the envisioned situation arose, those who were "lucky" were better prepared to make a decision in the moment.

- **They feel lucky.** This is despite any negative past experiences, whereas "unlucky" people allow past negative events to dictate future expectations. The lucky people also described their expectations of upcoming interactions with other people as generally positive. That is, they anticipate their own good fortune.

- **They deny bad luck.** Wiseman describes two primary ways people turn bad luck into good luck. Basically they interpret the bad as "could have been much worse." And, when they reflect on past events, they spend more time visualizing and selectively remembering the positive. In other words, the bad wasn't all that bad, and the good was pretty great.

Like Wiseman's subjects, we can all create our own luck by doing what people who consider themselves lucky do: position ourselves to have chance encounters that lead to interesting new possibilities and opportunities, see the upside of the experience, and harness the power of curiosity to be creative.

Living True to Ourselves

In her book *The Top Five Regrets of the Dying*, Bronnie Ware describes her years of experience working with patients in their final days.[18] As a palliative nurse, she cared for those who had often lived a long life and were reflective in their last days. As she recounts in her book, the number one regret her patients expressed was not being authentic and true to themselves—not daring to take on their dreams and challenges—and instead trying to live the life others expected of them.

It's not laziness and indolence that holds us back. It's an inability to overcome the fear of trying. Courage is not blindly facing the unknown and stampeding ahead anyway. Courage is instead carefully considering and recognizing the risks, obstacles, and opportunities before us and proceeding in measured steps despite these risks.

By carefully considering, and preparing for, each forward move, we mitigate risk and become stronger and mentally sharper with each step. But the stepping is critical. The starting means everything. When initiating an endeavor we have never attempted before, it's important to overcome fear and paralysis by making forward progress, however small. *Action creates clarity.*

Here's what I mean: you can think and envision and ponder and predict what will or might happen when you start that new business, give that big presentation, run that marathon, or take that trip to Madagascar. But you won't know, *really know*, what it's like until you start. Experience is invaluable, and making tiny adjustments along the way is required, which is why action creates clarity.

Consider the acrobats in a Cirque du Soleil show. Their tremendous feats of flying high above the arena are the result of hours and hours of careful and methodical training. We know this. But there was still a first time they leapt without a net. And there was still a first time that an Olympic skiing long jumper launched off a ninety-meter jump. And there was also a first time you gave a presentation in front of fifty people, or gave a formal report to your executive team.

The greatest leaders, and our dearest friends, cheer us on when we try something new.

Courage can be learned, and courage can be practiced. The more we practice risk, the more we are able to take risks.

Once we recognize, and believe in, the strength of our own growth potential, we can work on building our own self-confidence and the confidence of those around us, as we explore in the next chapter.

CHAPTER 2

Build Confidence

Confidence. That elusive *je ne sais quoi*. Like art, we know it when we see it, and we know it when we feel it. The thing is, confidence isn't summoned on demand from the heavens. Confidence isn't brought on by clenching our fists. So how do we achieve and sustain it?

We don't work in a vacuum, and mutual trust and confidence are at the core of successful teams. And building and maintaining confidence is not always easy; it often requires individual acts of courage. And while assuming the best in others is important to the process, obstacles—including stress-inducing bosses—can present challenges. But, if we are persistent, we can overcome many of these.

Sources of True Confidence

The world is full of people who have overcome daunting odds. In chapter 1, we explored how some people faced tremendous challenges. The question then is, "How did these people summon the confidence to attempt their audacious feats?" True and profound confidence comes from a lot of factors, as we explore next.

Preparation

If we eventually are rewarded publicly for our efforts, it's likely we spent years honing and practicing those skills in private before anyone noticed and applauded. Being prepared ranks as one of the strongest confidence measures among professional athletes and can give any of us confidence, whether on the sports field, on the stage, or at a workplace meeting. Preparation leads to competence, which in turn begets confidence.

Visualization

Recollecting positive performances in the past can give us a confidence advantage. When we take a moment to recall a time in which we were previously successful, we fuel a sense of confidence that we can repeat that success. Just as powerful is visualizing future success, as many high-performing professionals and athletes do.

In an interview with David Winner for ESPN, Wayne Rooney, a prominent English soccer player and team captain, explained that, before each match, he would approach the guy responsible for the team uniforms, the "kit man," and ask him the colors their team would wear for the game. Then Rooney would lie in bed the evening before the big match and envision himself performing well in the game. As Rooney describes it: "You're trying to put yourself in that moment and trying to prepare yourself, to have a 'memory' before the game. I don't know if you'd call it visualizing or dreaming, but I've always done it, my whole life."[1]

The deeper and more vividly we can visualize our future performance, the better. Nicole Detling is a sports psychologist with the United States Olympic team. As she notes in a *New York Times* article, "The more an athlete can image the entire package, the better it's going to be."[2]

Detling also coaches Emily Cook, one of the most accomplished athletes on the U.S. Ski Team. Cook's specialty is aerials—a sport in which skiers fling themselves into the air off of ski jumps and perform twists, turns, and flips in the air. In the article, Cook described the athletes preparing in the starting gate for the aerials competition at the Sochi Olympics: "Oh, yeah, it's ridiculous; we're all up there flapping our arms. It looks insane, but it works."

Great Coaching

Good coaches can instill confidence in many ways, but the greatest coaches are honest, specific, and positive, all at the same time. They're honest in that they don't ignore the behavioral or performance weaknesses of the people they coach but instead address those weaknesses head-on and provide correctional advice that is both specific and positive.

For example, if a person practicing a presentation constantly turns his back to the audience and reads bullet points, his coach might say, "You know your content. Turn and face your audience and smile. They can read your bullet points on their own. Or even better, tell your audience a story that illustrates the bullet points on the slide."

Innate Advantages

We're more likely to be confident if our team is bigger, faster, and stronger, but we need to avoid letting confidence become arrogance. And any team in a company that simply has more capacity and resources than the competition will likely enter proposal negotiations with more confidence.

Social Support

First-time parents, members of exercise clubs, cooking class attendees, and OCD group participants all get together for one purpose: to support one another through a specific change or toward a specific goal. When we feel a little lost or unsupported, that's a good time to reach out to those in our work or community who are experiencing the same pain point. No matter what we think, none of us is unique, and we can bet someone else is going through the same issue. Asking for help is the first sign of strength.

Competitive Advantage

In looking at our competitors, we may see that the sun is in their eyes, their lane is full of gravel, the field is tilted, or they simply have a crappy Internet connection. Recognizing such competitive advantages is a valuable source of confidence. The key is working hard to recognize the advantages we might have. This is when competitive sleuthing can be valuable in helping to recognize, and to articulate clearly what our advantages are.

Self-Awareness

Contrary to the old wisdom of using positive self-talk, such as "I think I can, I think I can, I think I can," to boost self-confidence, using positive questions is much more powerful. If instead we ask ourselves, "Can I do this?" we will have to answer the question in our minds and be specific about how we will meet the challenge.

I didn't make this up. Researchers asked a group of people to solve anagrams—puzzles in which the letters of one word are reshuffled to form another word, such as "team" or "meat"—but told participants that the study was looking at handwriting practices.[3]

"With this pretense," the researchers explained, "participants were given a sheet of paper to write down twenty times one of the following word pairs: Will I, I will, I, or Will. Then they were asked to work on a series of ten anagrams."

Those participants primed by writing "Will I" solved twice as many puzzles as the others. In being honest with ourselves and asking if we are up for a challenge, we're more likely to face that challenge successfully than simply repeating, "I think I can."

Self-Control

Studies have shown that practicing small, consistent acts of self-control can bolster confidence and self-esteem. Simple, small acts—such as avoiding sweets and candies, or consciously improving one's posture, or even practicing the routine discipline of keeping a daily diary—were all demonstrated to improve personal sense of self-esteem and confidence, according to studies by Mark Muraven at the University of Albany.[4] Muraven found that the specific self-control activity—avoiding sweets, improving posture, or keeping a diary—was less important than the act of self-control itself.

Through small acts of self-control in any activity, we can gain self-control in all we do. It's a self-reinforcing, positive feedback loop.

Trust

Trust could be the biggest factor in creating confidence in team settings. I once watched a dynamic youth soccer team whose members trusted one another crush a team of handpicked all-stars. The all-stars had been told that each of them was amazing, so they played like that. The kids on that team passed the ball as little as possible, and each selfishly worked for his own glory. The other team was a real team—one that had built strength, experience, and trust in one another over years of working together. They were never told that they were great individually. They had built their wins by always relying on one another.

Trusting and relying on others also works the other way around. When we have the trust to rely on others, we also accept responsibility for their reliance on us. Becoming a reliable teammate is absolutely a choice, in the same way that becoming more "engaged" in our work also starts with a personal choice.

Building Confidence Through Personal Acts of Courage

Even for those who can call on some, or all, of the factors discussed above, building confidence sometimes comes down to personal acts of courage.

"Seek small improvement one day at a time," UCLA Bruins Coach John Wooden famously said. "That's the only way it happens. And when it happens, it lasts."

I recently spent half a day working with executives from a global technology company. Our goal was to develop ways to heighten the engagement and drive of the company's team members. The twenty or so executives assembled that day were responsible for immense teams and for the work and livelihood of thousands of people around the world.

To kick things off, we reviewed results from a recent company-wide engagement survey. The results were so-so. While the ratings were fairly positive in response to the question of whether respondents were proud to work for a famous and well-known brand, the results were poor regarding levels of personal engagement and whether respondents felt the company leadership was open, accessible, and communicative.

Many respondents claimed communication was lacking between the higher and lower levels in the company, that they felt left in the dark, out of the loop. In an anonymous comment, one of the participants in the survey asked, "Now what are the executives going to do about the lack of engagement around here?"

So how do we solve this problem?

It Starts with Choice

There is a simple truth about people who become great leaders: they step up. It doesn't start at the top. We can't sit around and wait for the culture to change, or the engagement to start happening magically. We have to make it happen. It starts with each of us and our own personal attitudes and behaviors.

Yes, it is true that managers often define the personality of the company for the employees they manage, and that we experience the company through the quality of our relationship with our bosses. It's also true that the best way to attract outside talent is to have great managers.

But this doesn't absolve managers of the responsibility of being accountable, and being as present as they can be in their work. Each of us must accept responsibility for our own "engagement." Managers only create the circumstances and the opportunity for those they manage to do their best work.

Make It Easy on Yourself

The expression "activation energy" was coined 150 years ago by a chemist. The term refers to the minimum amount of energy required to stimulate an interaction between available reactants.

We should also minimize the amount of energy it takes to get us active—remove all the hurdles to taking action that we can. If we want to start jogging more, we should lay our gear and our shoes by the bed before we go to sleep. That way, it will be right there staring at us in the morning. And if we want to become better public speakers, we need to block off a doable amount of time—perhaps thirty minutes each day—to focus on that.

When we make it easy to begin something, we lower the amount of energy it takes to get started. And if it takes less energy to get started, we are more likely to do it.

It's Not Where but What You Think

Hip workplaces and free cafeterias are cool, but ultimately it's not where but what we think, and how we behave, that matters. For example, in April 2015, I had an interview with Paul Hiltz, president of Community Mercy Health Partners. I had previously interviewed him for my first book, *Out Think*, back in May 2011, when he was president of Mercy Health Select, and since then Paul has grown in his career and is now the president of Community Mercy Health Partners in Springfield, Ohio. In his new position, he heads the staff of two different hospital systems that have come together and moved into a brand-new, $500 million, state-of-the-art facility.

Over the course of several years leading up to 2015, the center had begun to create remarkable results: its emergency department wait times had plummeted from almost an hour to less than ten minutes; the rate at which discharged patients return soon after with the same condition, also known as "bounceback" rate, had fallen tremendously; and the center's surgery efficiency rating and surgery error rating were 30 percent better than the national average.

Thinking perhaps the new building was somehow inspirational to the staff, I asked Hiltz what role the new facility played in helping to bring about high levels of staff engagement and focus on patients. He explained that the new hospital, equipment, and facilities were all very nice, and definitely increased their ability to effectively treat patients, but they were not big factors in developing the collaboration and camaraderie of the staff.

In his opinion, the deep and meaningful collaboration and heightened patient care from his staff came from the conscientious work and collaboration of all employees, not from simply working in a fancy building.

Rehearse Excellence

Last year Odell Beckham Jr., wide receiver for the New York Giants, made what many argue to be the greatest wide-receiver catch of all time. When you watch it on YouTube, it looks like a magic trick out of Cirque du Soleil.[5] But here's the thing: he worked on that exact type of catch over and over and over in practice. He didn't just summon that move on the spot, unrehearsed. He spent many, many hours preparing for that exact moment.[6]

In practice, and before every game, Beckham warms up by attempting exactly these types of acrobatic catches. When the moment came in the actual game, he was exceedingly well prepared and practiced. He caught that ball because he rehearsed that difficult move, not because he got lucky.

Striking a Power Pose

Want to summon confidence quickly? Power posing certainly helps. As we learned, Harvard professor Amy Cuddy has spent the last few years of her life spreading the gospel of striking a power pose.[7] And it does work. When we stand like Wonder Woman or Superman, we get a shot of dopamine and oxytocin, which spreads a warm cocktail of confidence throughout our brain.

Cuddy recommends that, before a big interview or meeting, we go hide in the bathroom or elevator and do power poses. Doing this gives us a nice shot of confidence for a short period. But it's a stopgap—the duct tape of confidence.

The upshot is, go ahead and strike a power pose, but remember that real, sustainable confidence is found through developing competence. This is tough love, but nothing substitutes for hard work, perseverance, and dedicated practice.

Building confidence in ourselves and others also starts with small acts of trust and assuming the best intentions of others. The next story illustrates what I mean.

Assuming the Best Intentions of Others

A young woman is waiting in a busy airport. She has some time to kill, so she buys a little bag of cookies and sits down to read her book. Pretty soon, a young man comes and sits beside her and starts reading a magazine. The two people keep to themselves, and after a couple minutes he reaches into the bag between them and takes a cookie.

She can't believe it. I mean, seriously? The gall! But she's too astonished to say anything. So she takes a cookie and keeps reading her book. Time goes by, and she keeps reading and eating her cookies. But every couple of minutes this strange guy keeps reaching into the bag and taking a cookie until there's only one left. Then he takes the last cookie, breaks it in two and offers her half. She can't believe his guy! She stands up, and without a word to him, walks away and boards her flight.

Sitting in her seat on the plane she takes a deep breath to calm down. Then she reaches into her purse to get her book and finds the bag of cookies she bought earlier.

The moral, of course, is to be careful in making assumptions. Or better, always assume the best intentions of others. The following tools can help us meet this goal:

- **Practicing mindful listening**. Waiting to talk isn't listening. We all probably have had ineffective conversations before. We say something and, instead of acknowledgement or affirmation, we get back a completely different agenda because the other person was simply waiting for her turn to talk. Instead of just waiting for our turn to talk, we should listen carefully, then reiterate what the other person has expressed, but in our own words. This deepens the conversation, and the relationship. The other person is likely to say, "Yes, exactly!"

- **Focusing on behaviors, not people**. Instead of describing someone's personality (as abrasive, fun, mean, weird, interesting...) to ourselves and to others, we should stick to describing their behavior, and we should also not reduce them to stereotypes. People are complex, and each is unique. Their days are likely to be filled with stresses and joys, as are ours. We need to remember that moods change.

- **Honoring differences and disagreements**. We often have meaningless, small-talk conversations because they are easy. We all show up in the world with our own history, predispositions, and beliefs. And we know if we express those ideas we might create conflict and disagreement. It's okay. There's a difference between disagreeing and offending. When we set our defaults to listening and understanding, we are more likely to honor and learn from the differences among us.

While all this may sound simple, there is often a big gap between knowing the best thing to do and actually doing it. To build confidence in ourselves, we need to remember to assume the best in others. This small step can make a world of difference.

Building Confidence When the Boss Is Always Watching

While we should try to assume the best in others, sometimes bosses make that difficult.

According to researcher Robert Hogan, 75 percent of working adults today say the most stressful, most dreaded interactions they have at work is with their immediate boss. Stress-inducing bosses have even been linked to increases in illnesses related to heart disease,[8] with studies showing that the correlation of bad bosses and heart trauma seem to occur together.[9]

As a result, these same professionals avoid dealing with their bosses by hiding, often in plain sight—hiding in their e-mail, meetings, phone calls, commutes, and projects that "demand" their attention. And, with the current quest toward greater transparency, this hiding has become more difficult. This quest has spawned open work spaces and naked communication practices that approach surveillance levels—all in the pursuit of "visibility." Indeed, the seventh principle of "The Toyota Way" is "use visual control so no problems are hidden."[10]

Many bosses with good intentions believe that regular oversight will elevate performance, drive healthy competition, and enable them to tweak processes by watching workers from a higher vantage point. They think that, by studying worker activity, they can gently guide the team activity in the right direction toward higher efficiency and greater collaboration and productivity.

Yet Harvard professor Ethan Bernstein discovered almost the opposite. In a series of studies, he found that the greater the oversight, the lower the productivity and worker morale. He dubbed this phenomenon the "transparency paradox." What he discovered is that even modest levels of privacy for small groups of workers significantly increased productivity and engagement in their work.[11]

Organizational transparency can, of course, have very positive effects. It can enable increased awareness of the capabilities of other teams, and enable team members to more easily build cross-functional collaboration. These are clearly good things. And transparency in surfacing product or service issues can certainly isolate problems more quickly, enabling faster correction. Transparency can also help ensure that localized problems don't linger. As Justice Louis Brandeis famously said, "Sunlight is the best disinfectant."

However, in Bernstein's studies, the professor found that when transparency was applied as constantly observing workers it had a negative effect. Constant observation by bosses was not only a performance distraction but also severely discouraged employees from experimenting with processes and deviating from procedures. In other words, when every action we take is constantly monitored and scrutinized, we are far less likely to try something new, experiment, and come up with a better way of working.

To perform better, innovate faster, and be happier in our work and life, we need to try to build autonomy into our lives. We will also likely be more persistent and tenacious in pursuing our goals.

Building Confidence Through Persistence

Back in the early '90s, my friends and I used to go to a club in Charlottesville, Virginia, to see Dave Matthews and his band play. It was free to get in. One time we drove there, and the doorman asked for $5, and we were like, "What!? What a rip-off. It's just Dave."

During that same time period, I found myself president of the Student Activities Union at my college in North Carolina, a job that mostly required throwing parties and sometimes managing intramural sports leagues. I discovered that, if your job is to throw parties, people often recommend bands to you. A friend recommended some band from Columbia, South Carolina, I had never heard of, but he assured me they would rock the house. He told me to call Darius Rucker, a member of the band, so I did and asked him if his band, Hootie and the Blowfish, would come play at our school. He asked for a keg of beer to play, which seemed pretty reasonable.

Once I picked my head up to pay attention to popular music a couple of years later, Dave Matthews and Hootie and the Blowfish were playing stadiums at $200 a seat and touring the world. I realized what a sweet deal I'd gotten when I booked Hootie back in college.

But here's the thing: all of those blockbuster songs they were playing, such as "Ants Marching," "One Sweet World," "Only Wanna Be with You," and "Hold My Hand," they had been playing in little nightclubs for fourteen people back in the day—and they'd been playing those songs for years. They didn't get famous and *then* write hit songs. They wrote hit songs, and the world didn't know it until after they had played them, again and again.

This is the myth of "suddenly" becoming famous. We don't become successful overnight. We become successful as a result of showing up every day and putting in the hours, developing deep expertise, and finding our tribe over time. Or, as Will Durant summed up the wise philosophy of Aristotle: "We are what we repeatedly do. Excellence, therefore, is not an act but a habit."[12]

It's about grit. We implore our kids to persevere, to stay in the game, to try new ways of solving a problem. We encourage our colleagues to "fail faster" in expectation of an innovative breakthrough. We all just need to be a bit grittier. One parent in California had a Kickstarter campaign to develop a line of action figures for boys called "Generation Grit."[13] The project subsequently failed on Kickstarter, which, according to the project's founders, only deepened their resolve to get a little "grittier" to make it work.[14] (See more about applying grit to our work and life in chapter 3.)

But how do we instill stick-to-itiveness in our kids, and in our colleagues? There are a few clues in recent studies from Brigham Young University in which researchers followed 325 families with kids between the ages of eleven and fourteen over four years, examining the behavior of those families.[15] After examining parenting styles, family attitudes, and subsequent goals attained by the kids, the researchers concluded that three key ingredients consistently created higher levels of persistence:

- Supportive and loving environment
- High degree of autonomy in decision making
- High degree of accountability for outcomes

From research by Teresa Amabile, Harvard University, and others, we have known for some time that high levels of autonomy lead to more creative outcomes (see more on the value of autonomy in chapter 6). But here we see that high levels of autonomy also build the confidence we need to live up to our aspirations.

"When held accountable in a supportive way, mistakes do not become a mark against their self-esteem, but a source for learning what to do differently," writes Paul Miller, associate professor of psychology at Arizona State University. "Consequently, children are less afraid of making mistakes."[16]

As we've learned, when we make positive assumptions of others, we amplify not only their confidence but also our own. Assuming the best intentions of others is an act of confidence, and building our own, and others', confidence is a personal choice. And yet, it's not like flipping a light switch. Bolstering confidence takes constant, incremental, and intentional effort. Creating confidence is the result of applied effort and work.

As Stephen King put it: "Amateurs sit and wait for inspiration. The rest of us just get up and go to work."[17]

CHAPTER 3

Introduce Challenge

Having confidence in ourselves and encouraging it in team members helps to build a base of trust but is not enough to lead teams to continual innovation and growth. Our next small act is to introduce ourselves, and others, to challenging circumstances and projects to build and maintain high-performing teams.

By having the confidence to overcome small challenges in our daily lives, we are more ready to meet the larger challenges we face at work and in the rest of our lives. And if we can do that, we can influence those around us to also accept challenges that will lead to learning and growth.

Often, the difference between teams that are successful and those that are not is in the way we measure success. Focusing on performance, rather than learning, is common, but that emphasis is misplaced. What is important is not how many sales we make or how many innovations we come up with, but what we learn and how we embrace that process that keeps us on the path to innovation and success.

To maintain a challenging environment, we, as leaders, have to be on guard against complacency, an innovation killer. We also need to keep the fire lit under our team, reaching out to all members to make them feel they belong—that they are valued and we trust them to move us forward to success. And that also means embracing failure when it occurs in the face of meeting new challenges and trying new solutions. We should treat failure not as a character flaw but rather as a character *builder*.

Failure often ultimately leads to success, and helps build grit and resilience in those who face it and grow from it. Sometimes it's not the smartest person but the one who hangs in there despite all obstacles who wins and adds the most value to a team.

In building the best teams, and ultimately the best organization overall, we need to attract the top talent. Research has shown that, despite what some organizations think, employee engagement is not just about the money being offered but rather the chance to do meaningful, challenging work in an environment that encourages that and allows for failure. In offering such an environment, we are sure to attract and retain the best professionals, and ultimately build a successful organization.

Challenging Our Fears

What's one of your biggest fears? Spiders, maybe? Public speaking? Annual performance reviews?

Let's say it's snakes. Many people are terrified of snakes. Picture one now in your mind. Imagine that you are being asked to stand next to the snake. Now you are being asked to touch it, or even hold it.

Dr. Albert Bandura is ninety years old now and widely considered one of the greatest living psychologists today, and among the greatest ever, standing alongside B.F. Skinner, Sigmund Freud, and Jean Piaget. Bandura still practices in his office at Stanford.

More than forty years ago he began experimenting with helping people overcome their phobias, starting with people who were afraid of snakes.[1] These were people who had such a profound, paralyzing fear of snakes that they were terrified of even walking in a park or garden lest they come across one. Their phobia of snakes had truly become a limiting factor in their quality of life.

Bandura would bring the patient into his office and tell him that there was a snake in the next room, behind that door, and that he was going to go in there and touch it. You can imagine the reaction. Most patients told Bandura what he could do with that idea! There was no way on earth they were going in there. Ever.

First Bandura would have the patient stand behind a one-way mirror facing the adjacent room and look at a snake being held by a veterinarian. Patients would often panic, believing that the snake was going to suddenly attack and strangle the veterinarian. But instead, the handler held the snake comfortably and lazily.

Next Bandura would ask the patient to put on thick leather gloves and even a protective mask, if he wished, and stand in the same room as the snake. And finally, Bandura and his patient would gradually approach the handler and the snake. Over time, using this slow approach he called "guided mastery," his patients developed the ability to touch the snake with a gloved hand and ultimately even hold the snake in their bare hands—or, amazingly, allow the snake to crawl in their laps, with their hands idly at their sides. And just like that, the patient's phobia would be gone.

Bandura checked in with his patients in the days and weeks after they left his offices, and, universally, he discovered that their phobias stayed gone. One patient, long after her session with the snake, recounted having a dream in which a friendly boa constrictor helped her wash the dishes. Another patient was able to wear a necklace for the first time in her life. And another dramatically increased his real estate sales because he was no longer afraid to show rural properties.

In interviews after they'd overcome their fear of snakes, Bandura's former patients also revealed something more profound. Many reported that, once they had been cured of this debilitating phobia, they started trying other new activities. Some started doing public speaking, or taking more audacious risks in their professional work. One patient started horseback riding. In general, Bandura's patients reported feeling more free, less inhibited by fear.

Bandura's conclusion from his research was that, by destroying one fear in their lives, these people had begun to develop the mindset that they could change other paralyzing aspects of their lives as well.

When we begin to understand that we can challenge, and overcome, limiting ideas in our lives, we begin to strive for learning challenges instead of performance goals. Let me explain...

Shifting Goals from Performance to Learning

A performance goal is an aspiration to perform well. We want to shine. We want to be brilliant. We want people to applaud. We want to be amazing. We want the medal around our neck and the beaming joyful praise from those around us. A performance goal is tied to our ego.

A learning goal, in contrast, is an aspiration to learn something new or improve at a particular skill or task. Learning something new requires experimentation, hard work, long study, or new ways of collaborating. Learning goals are hard to achieve.

Sometimes a learning goal involves staring intently at someone else who is more skilled in order to visualize, and then develop, a particular skill. And sometimes a learning goal involves spectacular failure while attempting something new.

Carol Dweck, the author of *Mindset*, led a fascinating study in which she and her colleagues worked with 128 fifth graders (78 girls and 50 boys) and gave them a series of tests—mostly puzzles—then praised them in two different ways with just a few words.[2] The kids first were given a test that all of them did very well on. The researchers were confident before the test that these kids would do well.

Afterward, the researchers praised a third of the kids for intelligence, saying, "You must be smart at these problems." The next third of the group was praised for effort: "You must have worked hard at these problems." And the final third, the control group, was given no explicit praise for either hard work or intelligence.

The first word set praises intelligence and innate talent or skill. This is similar to the way many parents and coaches talk about kids. This is sometimes the way we speak to kids in performance situations. We tell them how smart they are, or how naturally gifted they are. We tell them they play piano like Mozart or paint like Picasso.

The second word set praises effort, determination, and hard work. After delivering two different kinds of praise, the researchers were interested in how the kids viewed their own abilities and what kinds of challenges they would choose for themselves.

In the next phase of the study, the researchers gave the kids another round of puzzles. But this time the kids were offered a choice. They could try harder problems or easier ones. As we might expect, the kids praised for hard work chose to attempt harder problems. After all, they were just told they did well because they worked hard. Why not try for the harder problems?

The kids praised for their natural talent and innate brilliance selected the easier problems. Why? Because when you praise for innate talent, you create a form of status. If someone believes she has special talent and is *expected* to perform well, then the thought of failing becomes scary. Therefore, to protect ourselves as "gifted and talented" individuals, we will choose easier tasks to ensure we have high performance. After all, no one wants to be revealed as an impostor.

In the next part of the study, all of the kids were given harder problems. And all of the kids performed poorly, although the kids praised for hard work spent more time on the test and did a little bit better. After the test, the scores were given out, and the researchers asked the kids to share their results with their classmates. After all, it was just an experiment. It didn't really count as part of their school-work. Who cares, right?

In sharing their test scores, the kids praised for talent lied just a little bit about them. They told their friends they did better than they actually did. Presumably, this was to maintain their social sta-tus as "talented."

However, when the kids praised for effort were asked to tell their peers how they did on this set of questions, a much smaller per-centage of them exaggerated their performance, feeling no loss of self-esteem when they did poorly on difficult problems.

"What's so alarming," Dweck says, "is that we took ordinary chil-dren and made them into liars, simply by telling them they were smart."

After the third round of difficult problems, the researchers asked the kids how willing they were to continue after such a hard test. They asked the kids to select, on a scale of one to ten, how will-ing they were to take another test.

As expected, those praised for intelligence were the least moti-vated to continue, and those praised for effort were most interested in continuing, with the control group falling somewhere in between.

In conclusion, Dweck and her colleagues looked at the choices the kids made after receiving the two different kinds of praise. I'll skip right to the punch line:

- Sixty-nine percent of the children praised for intelligence preferred performance goals.
- Eighty-eight percent of the children praised for hard work preferred learning goals.

That's right—when we praise for intelligence, we reinforce a predisposition to protect a "gifted and talented" status by choosing tasks at which we are more likely to perform well. And when we praise for hard work, perseverance, tenacity, and pluck, we reinforce the notion that learning is a good thing—that choosing difficult tasks for the sake of continuous improvement is something to be sought after.

A more recent study reveals that those who have a "fixed" mindset and believe they have a finite amount of intelligence also tend to overlook or ignore mistakes they have made.[3] In contrast, those who possess a "growth" mindset are more likely to correctly identify their own mistakes and consciously attempt to correct them.

When we see excellence, we should praise the effort, grit, patience, and hard work it must have taken to get there. We'll not only be rewarding excellence but also reinforcing the idea that continuous growth and learning is a good thing, and that challenges are to be embraced, not feared. Constant growth and learning is one of the key ingredients to building resiliency and overcoming difficult situations and setbacks.

Identifying a Company's Mindset

Companies, like individuals, have mindsets, and those mindsets can pervade the companies' cultures. The key to recognizing whether your organization's culture has a fixed or a growth mindset is to pay attention to the language the people in it use. In an interview, Carol

Dweck described the importance of recognizing the focus of attention and the language we use to describe ourselves and others.[4]

If the culture in the organization focuses on how smart or brilliant a person is, then the culture is reinforcing fixed mindsets. On the other hand, if people in the company are talking about who is enthusiastic or who is passionate about her work, that's a clue that the company is reinforcing a growth mindset.

Dweck also emphasized listening to the way people talk about failure, mistakes, and feedback. If they are hiding mistakes and only sharing them privately, that's also an indicator of a fixed mindset. Another indicator is being defensive about receiving feedback.

Turning a Fixed Mindset into a Growth Mindset

We absorb and adopt the mindset of the setting we are in. If we are immersed in an organization with a fixed mindset, we start to adopt that orientation ourselves. But there are ways to turn this around. We should start, Dweck suggested in the interview, by acknowledging the voice of the fixed mindset within us all.

Dweck recommends that if the voice of a fixed mindset inside our head is telling us, "You can still get out of here, or blame that guy for your failure, or hide your mistake" when we face challenges, we should acknowledge and respond to it. A constructive response to that voice in our head might be, "Well, you know, maybe I don't know how to do this, but all these people I admire have taken risks and they've come back from setbacks."

"I think it's really important for people to know that almost all of the great people that they admire, fabulously successful people, have had major, even monumental, setbacks that they've had to overcome," Dweck went on to explain. "And that that is part of the human condition, it's not part of being incompetent."

Dweck added that, when we talk back to ourselves with a growth mindset, we can come to the realization that adopting either a growth or fixed mindset is indeed a choice, and we have the power to make such a choice between the two.

This value of overcoming setbacks, and becoming more resilient by doing so, is demonstrated in the next story.

Making the Comfortable Uncomfortable

I coach lacrosse with my friend Pete Senger. Coach Pete, who played college lacrosse back in the day, certainly looks the part. Big, fast, strong, and possessing a booming voice, he seems like the kind of guy who would intimidate the new kids on the team, and only the seasoned players would dare to push his buttons or have the audacity to slack off during drills.

It's just the opposite. The new kids find him approachable, inviting, and encouraging as a coach. Yet the kids who have been playing with Pete for a few years find that he is sometimes demanding and expects excellence. He pushes those experienced players the hardest.

Pete has a coaching philosophy worth borrowing: "Make the comfortable uncomfortable, and the uncomfortable comfortable." What he means is that the new kids are already moderately intimidated by trying a new sport, developing new skills, and immersing themselves in the fast and often chaotic game of lacrosse. They are already on edge, perhaps even overwhelmed, and a bit past that learning state in which positive pressure creates excellence.

When the challenge and chaos of the game exceeds their skill and ability to deal with it, they feel overwhelmed and move from a state of thriving and learning to a state of retreat. They close down.

They drop a pass, take a hit going to pick up a ground ball, and can't figure out the confusing offside rule. The game suddenly isn't fun.

Inversely, the kids who have played the game for a few years have their posse, their attitude, and their predictable set of moves. These are the ones who need to try new things—who need to cradle and shoot with their nondominant hand, play a new position, and work on the face-offs that start the game. They need to get out of their comfort zone. They will learn to see more of the game and become better players.

Coaches like Pete are emotionally fluent leaders—those who can read people at their current comfort level and present just the right amount of challenge to let their skills and capabilities evolve. Sometimes, to accelerate excellence, circumstances need to be chaotic by design—intentionally unstable.

Working in a world of constant change is half the fun of it. Deadlines shift, goalposts move, budgets shrink, markets evolve, new competition emerges, perceptions alter, stakeholders clash, and, just when you are ready to deliver, your product is antiquated. After all, it takes a storm to make a rainbow.

Applying Grit to Our Work and Life

Long-distance competitive cycling is an actual sport. It's for a fairly small, and possibly loony, population of athletes, but it exists nonetheless. In May 2011, Juliana Buhring decided to ride her bicycle around the world.[5] She wasn't a cyclist, and she certainly had never been around the world. In her own words, she says she never intended to become a cyclist, she set out to cycle around the world.

On December 22, 2012, when Buhring completed her journey

and checked in at her home in Naples, Italy, she hoped to have logged the fastest ever female time around the world. It turned out, according to Guinness World Records, she was the first and only woman to do it.[6] Since then she has ridden her bicycle in races from London to Istanbul (the Transcontinental), and Oregon to Virginia (the Trans Am) each time finishing as quickly as the top male competitors.

But it's not her speed on the bike that distinguishes Buhring from her (mostly male) competitors, it's her perseverance in the saddle. She doesn't take as many breaks. It's like the story of the hare and the tortoise. She is simply willing and able to be tenaciously persistent in her task to ride her bike from point A to point B.

Buhring's mentor in developing her strategy was an endurance cyclist named Mike Hall. Hall told her she didn't need to ride fast, but simply take fewer breaks.[7] As with cycling, and many other aspects of life, speed doesn't necessarily pay off as much as sheer persistence and gritty determination.

Angela Duckworth and her colleagues have been studying perseverance and consistency as it relates to success and happiness in life. They have been quietly doing this research on "grit," a characteristic we introduced in the last chapter, at the Duckworth Lab at the University of Pennsylvania.

Years ago she and her colleagues started investigating why some people have greater success than others, without having greater intelligence or greater access to resources. Surveying the available research regarding traits beyond intelligence that contribute to success, Duckworth and her colleagues found it lacking in addressing the influence of grit, which they defined as "perseverance and passion for long-term goals."

"Grit entails working strenuously toward challenges, maintaining effort and interest over years despite failure, adversity, and plateaus in progress," they write. "The gritty individual approaches achievement as a marathon; his or her advantage is stamina."[8]

The researchers developed a gauge they call the "Grit Scale," intended to measure "grittiness"; respondents rate statements such as, "I have overcome setbacks to conquer an important challenge" or "I finish whatever I begin."[9] Through their work, the researchers at the Duckworth Lab have discovered that higher levels of grit correlate with higher levels of education, greater employment success, and even longer marriages. The results also showed that grit tends to increase with age, and that individuals with high levels of grit also tend to have fewer career changes.

Demonstrating how much of an effect grit can have on performance, the researchers found that those people identified as possessing high levels of grit often had high grades in school yet scored relatively poorly on Standard Achievement Tests, suggesting that, despite lower scholastic aptitude, their perseverance and tenacity yielded stronger overall academic results.

In a more recent study, Duckworth and her colleagues examined the correlation between grit and job retention.[10] Historically, studies have shown that job performance and retention is associated with five big predictive markers: emotional stability, conscientiousness, agreeableness, and, to a lesser degree, extroversion and openness to new experiences. Duckworth and her colleagues followed more than 1,100 sales representatives and found their level of "grittiness" directly correlated with their employment longevity.

When it comes to facing challenge in the workplace or at home, perseverance and a passion for long-term goals, plus a willingness to remain tenacious in the face of adversity, can make all the difference.

When we develop a growth mindset, we also become more resilient in the face of adversity and setbacks. The following story is just one great example.

Building Resilience Through Challenge

Considered one of the greatest speed skaters of all time, Dan Jansen was favored to win the gold medal in both the 500-meter and 1,000-meter races at the 1988 Olympics. Just a week before the Olympics, Jansen was on top of the skating world when he won the World Sprint Championships. He was fit and prepared.

As the day of the first Olympic race drew closer, Jansen's sister Jane was getting sicker and sicker, battling leukemia. In the early morning hours, the day of the 500-meter race, Jansen's sister died in a hospital surrounded by loved ones. Jansen was shocked and stunned as he deliberated whether to race. Believing his sister would want him to compete, he went to the track to warm up.

He said later that, in those moments he was warming up, he didn't even feel like it was himself inside his skin. He felt he had forgotten how to skate. In the 500-meter race, he lost an edge and went down just after the first turn. A couple of days later, in the 1,000-meter race, he again lost his feel for the ice, slipped, and went down.

Four years later, in 1992, in Albertville, France, Jansen was again on the ice ready to compete in the 500-meter and 1,000-meter races. Just two weeks before the Olympics, he had set a world record. He said he was superconfident he would win, and at the starting line he felt completely calm, without anxiety or nerves. Of his Olympic opportunities up until then, this was Jansen's time to shine. He knew there was no other competitor who could beat him that day. In the 500-meter race, Jansen took fourth place. In the 1,000-meter race, Jansen came in twenty-sixth.

Later, he couldn't explain his performance. He didn't fall. It was just as if he was skating as someone else. He wasn't nearly as fast as his recent times would have predicted.

In 1994, the Winter Olympics were held in Lillehammer, Norway. Jansen was at the peak of his physical health and his training, and this would likely be his last shot at an Olympic medal. Over the two years since the last Olympics, Dan had posted the five fastest times in history and was the only speed skater ever to break thirty-six seconds in the 500-meter race.

In that race, Jansen lost an edge on the final turn and slipped badly—not falling outright, but effectively losing the race. Now in his fourth Olympics without a medal, he was stunned and baffled, but not despondent. He later said he was confused, but he didn't despair. In his failure, he was disappointed but motivated. Instead of resignation, he felt inspired to succeed.

Jansen said that, when the gun went off for the final race of his Olympic career, he felt "incredible." He said that time slowed down, and that his efforts felt easy and instinctive. He felt as if he were in slow motion, with plenty of time to be hyperaware of his surroundings. Glancing up at the split times on the clock during the race, he saw that he was skating faster than he had ever before, in fact faster than *anyone* had ever skated. And he still had more in the tank. He won that race, and set a world record doing it.

He said the first thought that went through his mind at that moment was, "I finally skated to my potential at the Olympics." He had no idea yet if it was worth a medal or not. And he didn't care. On his victory lap, he carried his daughter Jane, named after his sister.

That final race was the culmination of years of preparation, resolve, and resilience. We need to remember to never be defined by a moment. Each event, and each day, is but another opportunity to meet challenges and fall forward.

Attracting the Best Talent

While we, as leaders, should always work to build up our teams by offering them challenges, we also should be on the lookout for the best talent we can add to those teams. Whatever industry we're in, our company faces competition from other companies. And the bigger and more successful the business is, the more likely it is to face competition. While the product we offer may be slightly different from similar products, with slightly different pricing, what makes brand X different from brand Y is the *people* in the company.

I recently started a new business building beautiful e-learning courses specifically so thought leaders, authors, and speakers could give greater reach to their ideas. I thought my idea was unique, one of a kind—that no one had ever thought of this before. Of course, I was wrong.

I only had to start talking about our new company to someone in the industry, and, sure enough, he would say to me, "Oh, that sounds a little like so-and-so. Have you heard of them?" And it's true, we do have competition, but our secret sauce is our people. Attracting and keeping the best people means continually offering them challenge, and the right environment in which to meet it.

According to research by the *Harvard Business Review*, 95 percent of high achievers near the age of thirty leave companies after only twenty-eight months.[11] Why? "For millennials, it is more a matter of career exploration than climbing the traditional ladder," says Emily He, chief marketing officer of the talent management company Saba.[12] It's about opportunity—the opportunity to find a workplace where we can reach our greatest potential and experience our greatest successes.

According to a new survey by Ernst & Young, of 9,700 full-time employees in the world's big-eight economies—the United States, Brazil, Mexico, the United Kingdom, Germany, India, China, and Japan—the top reasons (rankings varied slightly by country) are the following:

- Lack of opportunity to advance
- Minimal wage growth
- Excessive overtime
- A work environment that doesn't encourage teamwork
- A boss that doesn't allow flexibility[13]

It's the first item on the list I want to address here. Clearly, the data is telling us that talented professionals the world over are seeking career-development opportunities. Career development involves— often requires—challenge, and employees are citing professional growth among the top three requirements they need to stay at a company.

As I mentioned in the introduction to this chapter, the data suggests that retaining top talent is actually more complicated than simply giving aggressive pay raises, installing Ping-Pong tables, or offering to pay for night classes. None of this counts much if an organization's employees are constantly under stress. And these days, the entire professional business environment is stressful around the clock. From the time we wake up to check e-mail on our bedside smartphone to our marathon meetings and our search for a little "me time," we are under more duress today than ever before.

Consider, almost half (46 percent) of managers globally are working more than forty hours a week, according to the Ernst & Young survey. Millennials (64 percent) and gen Xers (68 percent) have the largest numbers of spouses working full-time as well— doubling the stress related to balancing home and child obligations.

Almost 70 percent of millennials and gen Xers claimed that "getting enough sleep," "finding time for me," and "balancing work and home life" were becoming problematic, according to the survey. And it's not just the American white-collar worker who is under stress. The survey results show that things are even worse in Brazil, India, the United Kingdom, Japan, and Germany.

I had an interview in June 2015 with Tom DiDonato, chief human resources officer at Lear Corporation. He says attracting and retaining top talent takes constant tweaking, and that there is no magic formula for balancing pay, flexibility, special benefits, educational opportunities, and early-release Fridays.

There is only one secret weapon, DiDonato says:

> Ultimately, people view the company through the lens of the person they work for. They don't say, "I work for Company XYZ, and even though my boss, and their boss, aren't role models for me, I really love the company." I doubt you will ever hear that.... If you view your boss as a role model, you probably think really well of the company. I believe that to my core. That's the one thing you don't have to tweak.... Keep getting great leaders. Keep developing great leaders. Keep having those people in your company that others view as role models, and you'll have that sustainable culture that attracts the kind of talent that everybody is vying for.

When we grow the greatest leaders from inside the organization, and keep them by offering them challenge and meaningful work, the strongest talent will come knocking at our door to work for them.

CHAPTER 4

Express Gratitude

While meeting challenges is valuable in building character, we also need to reward that effort. Expressing gratitude for good work is critical for trust and well-being in ourselves and in our teams.

Gratitude doesn't mean just saying "thanks." To show gratitude in a meaningful way, we must understand what drives our need for it, what drives us in our work and the rest of our lives. As we found in the previous chapter, it's not money that drives most workers; it's being able to do meaningful work, being challenged, and being appreciated. In this chapter we explore ways to stoke that feeling of being appreciated.

And while we all want to find meaning in our work, we also want to have fun. Having a sense of humor and encouraging others to express theirs can be a form of gratitude that helps build cohesion in the workplace and encourages everyone to strive for greater achievement.

Finding Gratitude

We touched on some of the ways we feel grateful for the work we do, but we need to dig deeper to really understand the source of that feeling before we can express our gratitude for the work of others and lead them on to greater accomplishments. We can start by exploring the effect on our sense of gratitude that making meaningful progress in our work and helping others can have.

Making Meaningful Progress

What drives you at work? I posed that seemingly simple question recently to a roomful of executives at a leadership retreat. No one budged. I offered some options:

- Is it the quarterly bonus?
- Is it simple praise and recognition from your colleagues and boss?
- Is it a sense that your colleagues have your back, that you'll get the support and resources you need in your work?
- Is it a clear sense of direction and goals—that your team knows where the heck it's going?
- Is it a sense that, day by day, you are making measurable progress in work that is meaningful to you?

They knew it was a trick question, because organizations have to get all of these factors right. Without fair pay, there is a deep sense of inequity and loyalty erosion. Without clear goals, people feel adrift and without purposeful direction. Without praise, people feel neglected. But one factor outweighs the rest—the last one: making meaningful progress.

As they wrote about in their book *The Progress Principle,* Harvard researcher Teresa Amabile and her colleague Steven Kramer analyzed twelve thousand diary entries from 238 employees in seven companies to come to the qualified conclusion that the most valuable work motivator is a sense that we are making progress in work that is meaningful to us.[1] When we signed up to run that marathon, we definitely had a clear goal in mind, but it was the daily effort in making incremental progress that kept us going. That quarterly bonus is nice, but we're not going to stay if that's all we're getting out of a job.

When Amabile and Kramer concluded that research in 2011, only 5 percent of leaders surveyed understood that meaningful progress is our most powerful motivator. I interviewed Amabile when *The Progress Principle* came out in 2011, and she said her goal was to tip that figure over 50 percent.

It's important to point out that, while praise, incentives, equitable pay, interpersonal support, and clear goals are all important, they are also all extrinsic motivators—they come from the outside, from someone else. A sense of satisfaction in making progress doing meaningful work is an *intrinsic* motivator. It's a sense of joy and satisfaction that comes from within.

Creating a sense of meaningful progress is something that's within our control. It doesn't require external validation or reward. Here are a few ways to stoke your sense of meaningful progress:

- **Express creativity.** We should go ahead and add a flourish—put our signature on it, make it our own. When we dig a little deeper and do this, we take personal pride and ownership of our work. It becomes meaningful to us personally.

- **Revitalize dormant relationships.** Nothing is as marvelous as gaining new insights from old friends to fuel our efforts. As Wharton professor Adam Grant says, when we take time to proactively reach out to those people in our work and life with whom we haven't connected in a while, we revitalize both parties.[2] That's because, while we probably have a rich history we can catch up on, we can also share our ideas and projects over the past year and accelerate each other's work.

- **Assume leadership.** We should take responsibility, step up. Assuming leadership can be terrifying, making us feel scrutinized, uncertain, and out of our element. And that's a good thing. Pushing ourselves to the edges of our capacity in leading meetings, projects, and interactions will help us grow as leaders. We need to keep in mind that people are cheering for us. It may feel like we are being evaluated and dissected, but the truth is that most people in the world assume best intentions, are grateful we stepped in to lead, and are cheering for our success and the success of the whole project.

- **Be of service.** Other motivators come from the outside, from someone else, but our most powerful motivator comes from within. The real question we should be asking is not "What can I gain?" but rather "What can I contribute?" Not "What can I get?" but "What can I give?" Not "How is this person hurting or even helping my goals?" but "How can I help this person achieve her goals?"

Above all, we should avoid comparisons. Most of us, if we wish to be smarter than everyone else, will fail, because someone will always have more degrees, more accolades, or a higher Mensa score. And if the goal is to be rich, we will forever feel poor, because someone will always be richer. If the goal is fame, we need only look to the Kardashians to agree there is no amount of personal disclosure that could keep up with them.

Aspiring to be a better version of yourself is a good thing, but comparing yourself with others isn't. Once we recognize that such comparisons are detrimental, it becomes easier to serve the work that needs to be done.

Supporting the Work

"The world," businessman and diplomat Dwight Morrow once wrote to his son, "is divided into people who do things and people who get the credit. Try, if you can, to belong to the first class. There's far less competition."[3]

Lisa Fischer might be the greatest contemporary female vocalist you have never heard of. When she tours with Sting, her voice is so powerful, Sting will often nod to her during shows and let her open up and take the lead. She will improvise long, beautiful passages of melody. Her voice is astonishing in range and power.

Fischer has also been the lead female vocalist on every single Rolling Stones tour since 1989, sometimes prowling the stage with Jagger and singing lead on "Gimme Shelter." She claims that, when she is emotionally and vocally in harmony with Jagger, the audience vanishes and she feels as if she and the band are the only ones in the stadium. And you've likely never heard of her.

"Some people will do anything to be famous," Fischer says. "And there are other people who just sing. For me, it's not about anything except being in a special space with people. And that, to me, is the higher calling."[4]

Judith Hill was in rehearsals with Michael Jackson when he died. She has been singing backup for years for Jackson, Prince, and numerous others.[5] You've likely never heard of her, either. Luther Vandross sang backup on the late David Bowie's hit "Young Americans." You know Luther Vandross. He made the big time. But many do not make it to the big time, nor do they aspire to.

Next time we have a great idea, we should give it away, give it to someone who can deliver on that idea even better than we might be able to. Playing that supporting role is an act of kindness. And, as we learn next, small expressions of kindness can have immense impact in the world.

Performing Small Acts of Kindness

In October 2014, I interviewed Gene Klein, an eighty-seven-year-old Holocaust survivor, born in Czechoslovakia in 1928. In our interview, he vividly recounted the horrors of the experience. The only time he became emotional and tearful was when he recollected small acts of kindness—a guard who gave him portions of food, inmates who gave him hope, or a German engineer who protected him briefly from hard labor.

Kindness can be one of the most powerful and enduring gestures we can make to others. I'll never forget feeling lost and alone at summer camp until a young counselor invited me to sit on his bunk and read *Jaws* with him. I'm certain that, wherever he is in the world, he has no recollection of it. But I do.

Kindness is hard-wired into the human genome. Researcher Michael Tomasello, who studies human behavior, demonstrated that infants and toddlers instinctively show concern and compassion for those in need or distress. In their study, Tomasello and his fellow researchers took fifty-six two-year-olds and divided them into three groups.[6] All groups witnessed an adult drop an object and struggle to pick it up.

One group of toddlers was allowed to intervene and try to help the adult. Toddlers in another group were held back from helping by their parents. The third group watched as another adult stepped in to help. The group that showed the highest distress and concern was the group that was restrained and not permitted to help. More than 90 percent of those toddlers who were permitted to help, attempted to.

Another thing: kindness is contagious. It turns out both positive and negative behaviors are contagious. Bullying begets bullying. Teasing begets teasing. But Nicholas Christakis and James Fowler have been studying community behaviors and found that prosocial behaviors spread much more rapidly than negative behaviors.[7]

Not only that, researcher David Buss studied ten thousand people in thirty-seven countries to figure out the most powerful attractor for those looking for a mate.[8] Money? Yes, somewhat. Beauty? Yes, it matters—more to men than women. Intelligence? Yes, it ranks right up there at number two.[9]

But the number one characteristic desired around the world by those looking for a long-term relationship was kindness and compassion to others. We should reach out and practice kindness every day. It will make us and everyone around us happier and healthier.

Looking Outside the Box

The promotion we just got? A beautiful sunset with our family? That's amateur stuff to be grateful for. The waiter just refilled our coffee? Oh, how considerate. We thank him. Now we feel warm and thoughtful.

Let's go deeper: try being grateful for losing a big contract, or our kid's soccer team getting crushed on Sunday. Good. Now even deeper. After we get dumped by a girlfriend because the relationship was truly toxic, we write her a heartfelt letter of appreciation and gratitude. We're getting there. We should try to see these events as precious gifts.

This is where the hard learning happens. This is where growth, development, and renewal happen. My friend Kirsten, who also coaches youth soccer, argues that the greatest team bonding, life learning, and development happen after the throes of humiliating defeat.

In a study on relative happiness, both accident victims and lottery winners interviewed a year after their respective experiences, testified to the same personal level of happiness.[10]

"It's easy to feel grateful for the good things," writes Robert Emmons, codirector of the Expanding the Science and Practice of Gratitude project at the University of California, Berkeley. "No one 'feels' grateful that he or she has lost a job or a home or has taken a devastating hit on his or her retirement portfolio."[11]

If we can summon the strength to reframe a negative experience into a positive one, we can grow in our own self-development. If a relationship really was toxic and we have the strength to see through the emotional pain of being dumped to be grateful that the other person was willing to confront it and end the relationship, then we can grow and move on.

The beggar on the street can show us how privileged we are. The cancer that infected our body can show us how grateful we are to be healthy. When we summon gratitude in the face of adversity, we turn meaningless cruelty into growth and strength.

Increasing Engagement by Appreciating Others

Expressing appreciation for someone in our life can change our whole outlook. That's right—simply telling others how much we appreciate them will improve the way we feel.

Jeffrey Froh, professor at Hofstra University, did this cool study in which he and his colleagues tracked students in eleven different classrooms, dividing them into three groups.[12] For just a few minutes each day they were asked to do the following:

- Group 1—write down things they were grateful for at home and school
- Group 2—write down things they found to be a hassle and not fun
- Group 3 (the control group)—do nothing

Here are a few things group 1 wrote down:

- "My coach helped me out at baseball practice."
- "My grandma is in good health, my family is still together, my family still loves each other, my brothers are healthy, and we have fun every day."
- "I am glad that my mom didn't go crazy when I accidentally broke the patio table."

After two weeks, the researchers measured their subjects' school performance and engagement from both the student's perspective and the perspective of their teachers. Essentially, they found these students to be happier (by their own account), to have more friends, to be more engaged in their schoolwork (by the teachers' account), and...wait for it...they got better grades—compared with their own previous performance. That's after only two weeks. The researchers checked three weeks later, after the study was over, and found the effects were still present.

The effect is even more powerful when we share our appreciation with someone directly and personally. As described by Po Bronson and Ashley Merryman in their book *NurtureShock,* in a powerful follow-up to Froh's study, students were asked to write a letter to someone in their life whom they felt they may have never properly thanked.[13] The person could be a teacher, a coach, or a family friend.

The kids worked on their letters three times a week for two weeks. They were asked to elaborate on their feelings, and to be increasingly specific in their writing about what the benefactor did that they were grateful for.

On the Friday of the second week, each kid set up a meeting with the person to whom he had written his letter to read the letter to the person, out loud, face-to-face.

"It was a hyperemotional exercise for them," Bronson and Merryman quote Froh as saying. "Really, it was such an intense experience. Every time I reread those letters, I get choked up." The positive outlook and heightened engagement were still present when the researchers checked in with the kids two months later.

What if we can't easily get our kids to write a letter of gratitude to someone in their life? Here's a simple trick to get anyone thinking and reflecting about others who have made a profound and measurable impact in their lives. Just ask them to finish the following sentences:

- Someone who helped me get through a difficult time is _____.
- Someone who helped me learn something important about myself is _____.
- Someone with whom I can discuss the things that matter most to me is _____.

Sending a note of appreciation to someone who has had a positive effect on us can have a big impact. Picking up the phone or tracking down our supporter in person to thank her can have an even bigger one. Such a small act of appreciation not only can make that person's day but also makes us feel better about ourselves.

Now let's take a slightly harder step by not only appreciating the positive people and events in our lives but also the nasty and unpleasant ones.

Healing Through Humor

Forty years ago Norman Cousins, editor of the *Saturday Review*, had been given six months to live. As he wrote in his book *Anatomy of an Illness: As Perceived by the Patient*, he'd been diagnosed with a painful, degenerative disease of the spine.[14] Although Cousins was in constant agony and succumbing to paralysis, he checked himself out of the hospital (which he deemed "no place for sick people") and moved into a hotel.[15]

He began taking high doses of vitamin C and prescribing himself a regular regimen of intense laughter. Watching Marx Brothers videos and stacks of other funny movies that were among his favorites, he laughed and laughed every day. He discovered that the periods immediately following intense laughter had the strongest effect in easing his pain and calming his mind. Cousins recovered from his illness and went on to write several books on the healing power of laughter.

Even though constant disruptive laughter is the bane of every elementary teacher, the benefits of laughter are now well known. It wasn't always that way. There were times in the past in which laughter was frowned upon. "In my mind there is nothing so ill-bred as audible laughter," Lord Chesterfield, a British public advisor on morality, proclaimed in the mid-eighteenth century. In 1903, psychologist William McDougall wrote that situations that incite laughter are essentially unpleasant.

But we now know that laughter increases blood flow, reduces stress, decreases risk of heart attacks, and boosts the immune system.

Even the insurance giant AIG ran TV ads proclaiming that laughing will add eight years to our lives. And that information comes from their insurance actuaries, who should know.[16]

If the path to appreciating adversity is too great to surmount, or if the searing pain of defeat and rejection is just too powerful to allow us to be reflective and generous of spirit, we should let humor guide us. When we're lost in the woods, have run out of water, and nightfall is approaching, we should tell a joke—because humor heals. It combats fear.

Humor has the power to disengage our fears and relax us. Behind a nervous chuckle is the sentiment, "We're gonna get through this!"

Even dark humor might be just the right antidote. Try what world-class adventurer Erik Weihenmayer calls "positive pessimisms." In his book *The Adversity Advantage*, he gives an example: "We'll be sitting out in a raging storm. We've gone a month without showers. The wind is driving snow directly into our faces, and... Chris will look up with a big cheesy smile on his face and say, 'Sure is cold out here... but at least it's windy.'"[17]

As Weihenmayer describes it, it's a way of saying, with humor, that we all understand this is a grim and possibly dire situation, we are all suffering together, and yet we will also persevere together.

CHAPTER 5

Fuel Curiosity

Challenge and curiosity go hand in hand. Firing up both in the workplace paves the road to innovation and to happy, productive teams that are more likely to reach their potential for success. It's easy to settle into thinking everything is on track, but is what we're seeing just an illusion?

We shouldn't be afraid to challenge assumptions made within our organization and be relentlessly, assertively curious, not letting ourselves or others dampen our quest for answers. We should also inspire curiosity in others and avoid complacency. The results can be surprising—and highly productive.

Seeing Past the Illusion of Success

Here's an old brain trick: look at the illustration at the top of the next page. Which line is longer? You know this trick. They are the same, right?

Figure 5-1 *The Müller-Lyer illusion: which figure is longer?*

In taking off the fins, we dispel the illusion:

Figure 5-2 *The Müller-Lyer illusion: the lines are shown without the ends.*

Now we can see the difference in length, 10 percent, more clearly:

Figure 5-3 *With the lines closer together, the 10 percent difference in length becomes more apparent.*

Maybe you weren't fooled because you anticipated a trick. A curious mind might have tried to hack the trick and see through the illusion, which was named for German sociologist Franz Carl Müller-Lyer in 1889, who created it. Even when you know it's a brain trick—a visual illusion—it's still hard to see it differently.

While we can mentally adjust to what we think we see, it's much harder to adjust or change what we think we know. Such cognitive illusions can be more persistent and harder to dispel than visual ones.

Years ago, the psychologist Daniel Kahneman was invited to give a lecture at a financial-management firm that specialized in managing portfolios of very wealthy clients. In his book *Thinking Fast and Slow*, he writes that, before his presentation, he was given a spreadsheet that reflected the previous eight-year investment performance of the top twenty-five financial advisors at the firm.[1] Each year's performance was the basis of each advisor's yearly bonus. The better the return, the higher the bonus. Using the data, Kahneman could easily compute the correlation coefficients between the advisor rankings in each pair of years—comparing year one with year two, then year one with year three, year one with year four, and so on—for each advisor at the firm.

Kahneman anticipated that he would find only small differences in persistence of trading skill over the years among the top twenty-five advisors. But what he found instead exceeded even his own expectations. The average of correlations comparing all advisors' performance over an eight-year period was only 0.01, or effectively zero. In other words, the firm believed it was providing bonuses based on trading skill, but in fact the data showed nonexistent, or negligible, difference in skill among the top twenty-five advisors. The firm was clearly rewarding luck, not skill.

Armed with this bomb, Kahneman gave his presentation to the executive team. He thought the financial executives would be shocked and astonished to discover that there was virtually zero statistical difference in their skill as traders, and, furthermore, that their own reward system was based on a fallacy.

The reaction of the executives was instead blasé. It was as

if he had reported some obscure statistic that was irrelevant to their work. The audience clearly believed the results that Kahneman presented—how could they dispute facts? But they reacted as though the information were peripheral or entirely unrelated to their work, as if it were meaningless and extraneous.

The reason is the illusion of expertise, or what Kahneman calls the "illusion of validity." When we, as highly trained experts and professionals in our field, are presented with information that is contrary to our deeply ingrained experience or way of doing things, we ignore or invalidate the information. We dismiss the finding as extraneous and unconnected. And these persistent beliefs are further reinforced by the professional cultures we work in.

The point here is that people and teams with high levels of confidence, when highly subjective and reinforced by homogenous cultures, can be unreliable in terms of accuracy. When weighing a decision, we should not only get second and third opinions but get them from different perspectives and areas of expertise. Or, as Harvard professor Daniel Gilbert advises in his book *Stumbling on Happiness*, it's far better to get advice from people who have actually experienced what you are contemplating.[2] But, as Gilbert explains, this can be especially difficult, because we tend to believe that we are special and therefore we know what will satisfy us better than someone else, even someone who has lived through the very same decision-making events that we are contemplating.

The only way to gain new ideas by soliciting the advice of others is to ask questions to which we honestly don't know the answer. When we do ask someone else for advice, it's also important to thoughtfully consider their answers, instead of discounting them. We can start with the small act of listening intently and trying to learn something new instead of simply waiting for our turn.

Asserting Our Curiosity

You can spot a real expert versus a phony. Look for three little words: "I don't know."

Phonies will have all the answers, while experts will be willing to admit what they don't know. Real experts are relentlessly curious, even *assertively curious*—that is, they will demand explanations for things that many others simply accept as rules.

Creativity consistently ranks among the most sought-after and valued characteristics of workers today. Executives know that the next killer app, product, service, or innovation is going to come from relentlessly curious and creative people. The most desirable professionals today are happy, collaborative, and have hustle, but, above all, they are relentlessly curious and creative.

In a September 2015 study, the pharmaceutical company Merck surveyed more than 2,600 people on the value of creativity in the workplace and the ways in which the company encouraged (or stymied) creative practices.[3] While a staggering 90 percent agreed that the best ideas come out of persistent and curious behavior, including constantly questioning company practices, fewer than 25 percent of those working today described themselves as curious people.

We are more likely to call ourselves "organized" or "diligent," or even "friendly," than to call ourselves "creative." If anything, creativity is becoming even more scarce in this highly demanding work environment. According to a study by the software firm Adobe, more than 80 percent of us say the pressure to be more productive is increasing in intensity.[4] As work pressure builds to be more productive, our work environments increasingly stifle imagination.

Here's an interesting fact about people who describe themselves as curious and creative: these people are also assertive. Curious people are decision makers. They are influencers. In interviews, they often say they have direct influence over the outcome of decisions and change.[5] If you think of the people in your company and community who consistently drive change, I bet you will be thinking of inquisitive people—people willing to ask the hard questions.

That may seem counterintuitive. After all, if we are busy questioning the world around us, aren't we in a listening and receptive mode, and not in a decisive, action-taking mode? But these two behaviors—deeply questioning and then taking action—reinforce levels of creative engagement. This is because highly creative people also tend to be fearlessly persistent. They often describe themselves as "adventurous" and "risk taking."

Another characteristic of highly curious and creative people is that they are generally less affected by peer pressure. They tend to follow their values, even when their path runs counter to what the group is doing.

These tendencies toward curiosity and assertiveness start when we are quite young, and should be carefully guarded and sustained throughout our lives to constantly nurture a growth and learning mindset.

Reaping the Rewards of Persistent Curiosity

One day our daughter, Annie, and I were at a drugstore picking out a card for her to send to a friend. She was seven years old at the time. In the card display was a big section dedicated to Taylor Swift. We examined each card—Taylor Swift looking dreamy, sassy, alluring, or even defiant. Taylor can certainly strike a pose. I asked Annie to pick one.

"I can't decide," she said . . . then, "Wait, what about that one?"

It was the display poster, the marquee advertising the Taylor Swift section of the greeting cards. "Well, that's not for sale, sweetie," said the sales clerk we asked. "It's just the banner—you know, the poster for all the Taylor Swift cards."

Turning to me, Annie says, "Yeah. Can we get it?"

There was also a little sign saying the Taylor Swift card collection was being replaced in a few days. I shrugged. "Let's ask," I said. I took the poster from the wall, and Annie carried it to the checkout counter.

"I can't find a price on this," the clerk said.

I replied, "Yes, well, we know it's . . . ah . . . the display poster. But the sign says you are getting rid of the cards in a couple days. Can we have it?"

The clerk frowned. "I need to talk to the manager."

We waited, and the manager arrived, looked at the poster, and said, "I'm sorry but we don't own those banners. The card company does. We can't give them away."

I turned and saw Annie's face wrinkle in confusion. "But why not?" she asked.

For a second, no one moved. Then the manager said, "Tell you what. If you give us your phone number, we'll ask the card company and call you if they say you can have it." I was pretty skeptical, but Annie's face lit up and she carefully wrote down our phone number for the manager as I said it out loud.

We drove home, and I forgot all about it. But Annie didn't forget. Sure enough, about ten days later, the drugstore manager called and asked if we still wanted the poster. Within the hour, that Taylor Swift poster was hanging in our daughter's bedroom.

What did my daughter teach me from this? When in doubt, ask.

People who are seen by others as getting assertiveness right often mistakenly think they've gotten it wrong. In a 2014 study by doctoral students at Columbia Business School, 57 percent of those who believed that they were appropriately assertive in their requests and negotiations were actually seen by the other party as not adequately assertive or demanding.[6] In other words, more than half didn't ask for enough.

On the other hand, those who believe that they have been overly assertive and demanding in their requests and negotiations often fall victim to a belief that they have "crossed a line" and gone too far in their requests. The result is that they backpedal, try to smooth things over, and acquiesce to a lesser deal.

That's a bummer, because in the study those who were assertive and demanding were often interpreted by the other party as fair and appropriate.

According to the research, we should go for it and ask for a little more—and not back off or feel badly about what we ask for. This sense of assertive curiosity can be fueled by creating environments in which we constantly seek to suppress any tendency to be impressed by our own power and prestige, and instead seek to empathize and understand our teammates and colleagues.

Cultivating Curiosity by Shifting Perspective

"When you become successful is when you should be especially wary that you're about to become an idiot," says Bob Sutton of Stanford University. "And there's a lot of evidence to support that."[7]

Remember, our goal in this chapter is to focus on nurturing curiosity, within ourselves and in those around us, demonstrating that fueling creativity in others is a small act of leadership that will eventually lead to big impact, driving innovation for our entire organization. There is good evidence to suggest that our own success can stifle the curiosity of those around us, so it's important not to get too inebriated by our own sense of power and prestige. A powerful antidote to power poisoning is learning to take the perspective of someone else, to set aside our own agenda for a moment and consciously attempt to understand another's point of view.

One way to fuel the creativity of those around us is simply to work on understanding, and communicating back to them, their own perspective.

Robert Litchfield, associate professor at Washington & Jefferson College, has been studying the link between individual creativity, team dynamics, and the way management interventions psychologically affect people in organizations. He and his colleagues started their study, "Linking Individual Creativity to Organizational Innovation," with the premise that individuals all possess their own perspective, and those perspectives are not, of course, always the same.[8] For example, the restaurant investor will have a different perspective from the restaurant manager, and again a different perspective from the restaurant waiter.

The literature is full of studies on and references to failed communication and failed innovation, because it's difficult to both understand and align disparate perspectives—particularly from people operating in different departments in an organization. Litchfield's hypothesis at the outset of the study was that, if we could create a mechanism in which individuals were free to express their ideas, and were willing and encouraged to understand another's ideas, innovation would follow more readily. The researchers called this mechanism "perspective taking."

Perspective taking is the exercise of intentionally shifting from trying to convince others of an idea to trying to understand the ideas and perspectives of others. As the researchers note, perspective taking is an imperfect act, but evidence suggests that it often produces greater cooperation between individual perspective takers and those whose perspectives are taken.

The exercise of conscientiously taking another's perspective tends to elevate communication and openness to new ideas, because other team members feel a greater sense of empathetic interest. Those team members who exercised perspective taking also learned how to more effectively communicate new ideas to the team, because those members were better practiced in understanding the perspectives of others.

The formal hypothesis of Litchfield and his colleagues, which they later demonstrated, was, "The association between individual creativity and organizational innovation will be stronger when individual perspective-taking is high than when it is low."

In the experiment, they surveyed 146 triads (teams of three), each composed of a focal employee (the experiment target), a coworker, and a boss. Then each person was asked to evaluate four variables: how creative that focal employee was, how well he or she took others' perspectives, how creative the team he or she worked on was, and how innovative the organization was.

Their results were straightforward: "We found evidence that when individual creativity is high, the combination of individual perspective-taking and a highly creative team environment strengthens its link to organizational innovation."

As Litchfield and his colleagues demonstrated, the small, intentional act of seeking to understand another's perspective has a direct and powerful effect on accelerating collaboration and innovation.

Inversely, when we become intoxicated by our own sense of importance and inebriated with an inflated sense of self-importance and power, we tend to belittle—or ignore—the ideas (and even presence) of those around us.

In a study illustrating the intoxicating effects of a sense of elevated importance, social psychologist Paul Piff, at the University of California, Berkeley, and his graduate students discovered that people who drove fancy, expensive cars were far more unlikely to yield to pedestrians at a crosswalk.[9]

Piff and his students monitored hundreds of vehicles over many days and recorded whether or not they yielded. Fifty percent of those vehicles classified in the most *expensive* category (BMWs, Mercedes, Porsches, etc.) failed to yield, while none of the vehicles classified in the most *inexpensive* category broke the law at the crosswalk.

This is not to say that, universally, only rich people are prone to breaking minor laws but rather, Piff described in his research, that we all have competing motivations throughout our lives. In fact, it's not wealth alone that prompts individuals to believe they are above the law but rather the power disparity between themselves and those around them. According to an article on the Workplace Bullying Institute website, power disparities in the workplace have been directly correlated with workplace bullying, pay inequities, and even sexual harassment.[10]

According to Piff, "Small psychological interventions, small changes to people's values, small nudges in certain directions can restore levels of egalitarianism and empathy." He suggests that little but consistent prompts and positive social cues can make a big difference. He and his colleagues have discovered that small interventions, such as listening to a story depicting childhood poverty, remind us of the existence of social inequity in the world and restore empathetic behavior.

But as we explore next, once we understand and nurture the curiosity of those around us, sometimes we also need to let go.

CHAPTER 6

Grant Autonomy

Most people don't like someone always looking over their shoulder or second-guessing them. While it's good to help our teams build their confidence and meet challenges, it's also important to let them loose to explore and try their ideas on their own. When we feel like we own much of what we do, we tend to take responsibility and really love our work. And when we love our work, we learn faster.

Real learning rarely comes from success. It's the failures that really force us to ponder the details of what we do, to understand the things and processes we work with. Failure can also spur us to try and try again to actualize our ideas. The same is true when, as teammates or bosses, we allow others to fail. If we believe in our team and help them believe in themselves, we should also be confident that they will learn from their experimentation and go on to successes that may be even greater than we hoped for.

We also shouldn't let bosses ruin our initiative. Among the issues of autonomy we explore in this chapter is how to keep that from happening. Another is what we do when we fail, or when our work situation is intolerable. When should we quit, if ever?

Learning Faster When We Love It

Practice doesn't make perfect. There is no perfect. Great practice will hone good habits and get rid of bad habits. Poor practice is when we practice our mistakes over and over until they're ingrained.

By now, most of us have read, or heard of, the ten-thousand-hour rule, in which ten thousand hours is the magic practice barrier after which we get to be experts and gurus. Unfortunately, that has been a misrepresentation of the work of K. Anders Ericsson and his colleagues from Florida State University from the 1990s.[1] Ericsson never claimed ten thousand hours constituted the magic expert barrier.

However, research does support the idea of reinforcing "time on task." In sports, most today believe the best coaching and training involve increasing the number of "touches on the ball" instead of an older style of coaching in which players stand around watching a demonstration and then take turns doing one activity. Kids standing in lines indicates a poor practice; a good practice has everyone involved.

We learn by watching, but we learn faster by doing.

In 2014, a team of researchers examined eighty-eight different studies on the effects of practice over time and concluded that practice does count, but much less than previously argued.[2] Practice certainly matters, they found, but other factors were equally important, such as the participants' age when the activity was introduced and how much they enjoyed the activity. In one example, children displayed *thirty times* higher reading comprehension when they reported enjoying the reading.

That may come as no surprise, but we should keep that in mind when making project and task assignments in our professional work.

Task invitations that are a stretch but that people might enjoy are invitations for excellence. But we are far more likely to get mediocre results when we offer project and task invitations for activities people detest. And research seems to suggest that no amount of arguing for pluck, grit, and perseverance will improve results when the task presented is against the skill set of those assigned it.

I discussed this issue of granting autonomy with Scott Turicchi, CFO of J2, a $500 million technology company, in November 2015. He told me he very intentionally moves team members to different positions within his organization so they have the benefit of seeing different sides of projects and understand the greater picture of any particular project or deal in the works.

As Turicchi described, there's an even more important reason, greater than job experience and perspective, for working in different roles: finding the intersection of what we are good at and what we love to do. Turicchi said that the kinds of people he likes to hire are those who have passion for their work.

Once we've created a safe environment for people to explore their capabilities, we also need to let them fail on their own sometimes without our constant intervention, as we see in the next story.

Letting Others Fail on Their Own

Things were getting out of hand. It was time for an intervention. It was the end of 2014, and only a year earlier my wife and I had a thirty-minute "screen time" media option for our three kids. After homework, after chores, after mealtime together, and after checking in and sharing their daily activities with us, our kids could zone out on Netflix, Instagram, TV, or whatever they wanted for thirty minutes. In fact, this turned out to be a rather enjoyable time for us as well. While kids blanked out on devices, we could chat in the kitchen as we cleaned it up after dinner.

A year later the thirty-minute option had devolved into our kids leaping into one-, then two-hour headphone-wearing journeys silently watching *Parks and Recreation* or lost in Taylor Swift albums or bingeing on FIFA Soccer on Xbox—each drifting quietly to separate corners of the house.

I'm all for music and movies, and sometimes throw dance parties with the kids in the living room or have sessions of watching *Forrest Gump*, laughing together with the kids. But this had gotten out of hand. The rules had lost meaningful consequences, and often my wife and I were too exhausted to marshal the strength to stop it. It was time to break the habit.

Our experiment hasn't been consistently effective, but instead of demanding they adhere to the thirty-minute option or confiscating their devices, we've made progress when we've tried other approaches. We started initiating play with our kids, such as skiing over a ski jump we built, or playing soccer in the backyard. Or we assign the kids small jobs, such as setting the table or preparing parts of dinner. Or we simply explain that staring at a screen near bedtime makes it hard to go to sleep. When all else fails, I quietly go into the basement and unplug the Wi-Fi router.

That decision—to unplug the Wi-Fi—made the choice for them. In that moment, as a parent, I decided what was best for them. But as we learned earlier from the Brigham Young study, when we give our kids greater autonomy, responsibility, trust, and unconditional support, they tend to make more conscientious decisions.

Believe me, this certainly doesn't always work. In our experience, a fourteen-year-old does not always make thoughtful and conscientious decisions when granted autonomy. That's the understatement of the week, but it should be the eventual goal, because, in a few short years, he will be making many of these decisions without us around.

The same philosophy we used in granting autonomy to our kids extends to the workplace. Too often, hiring managers and recruiters brag about only hiring the best and the brightest from the top schools, but then won't give them the latitude to make even the most mundane decisions on their own.

In a November 23, 2015, interview, Bashar Nejdawi, executive VP of Ingram Micro, told me that sometimes he knows a project or initiative of a junior team will fail.[3] He has the experience and the insight to recognize that it's likely to bomb, but he lets it unfold anyway. He believes that, as long as it's not a mission-critical failure, it's more important to let people go through that learning experience themselves. They need to have the experience of understanding firsthand that a particular process or initiative won't work.

This boss understands that at some point we have to let go of those we manage, that the benefits of granting autonomy can yield big results in terms of company success. But what if the boss is more of a "bosshole," creating a toxic work environment where autonomy is in short supply?

Dealing with a Difficult Boss

Every evening, all around the world, many of us come home from work, greet our partners and our kids, and have discussions. Discussions in the kitchen, at the dinner table, and before we go to bed.

Sometimes the topic is school grades, or upcoming trips, or what to bring to the Lowensteins' barbecue. But often the subject of these discussions is the company we work for, our colleagues, and our bosses. It's long been known and understood that the quality of our work culture and of our relationship with our bosses can affect our mood, our sense of optimism or despair at work, and even our health.

Toxic work environments, and in particular cruel bosses, have been linked to hypertension, elevated blood pressure, and even heart attacks. One woman I worked with in recent years had kidney stones clinically attributed to the stress of her work environment.

Toxic bosses are also responsible for the disposition of entire teams when they single out individuals for criticism. When a boss pulls a person aside quietly and privately to deliver critical or disparaging feedback, that individual absorbs the critical evaluation and then infects the rest of the team. According to recent studies replicated with teams in China and the United States, each individual criticized subsequently becomes toxic and divisive to other team members.[4] It's true that negative attitudes are contagious.[5]

Seven in ten Americans say bosses and toddlers with too much power act similarly, according to one study.[6] In the study, 345 white-collar office workers described the most abusive and disruptive bosses in their lives as self-oriented, stubborn, overly demanding, interruptive, impulsive, and prone to throwing tantrums.

In such cases, mental jujitsu—the use of the strength or weakness of an adversary to disable him—could come in handy:

• **Give him credit.** If a boss needs to be "right" all the time, we should let him. I don't mean letting him sabotage a project by pushing it in a ridiculous direction, but rather practicing deep listening. We listen carefully to the boss's ideas, and reiterate them back carefully to clarify what we heard. In the retelling, our boss may, or may not, understand the fallacy of his reasoning. But, either way, he was heard and acknowledged.

- **Bring her down to earth.** If a boss paints grand visionary ideas without understanding the detail and the effort involved, we ask her to get granular, into the details. Help her understand how her great, sweeping vision plays out at the execution level of technology, marketing, and product redesign. Ask her who, specifically, she envisions doing this work? What resources might need to be made available to cover contingencies, or to hire outside help? When you help the boss understand the real effort involved, she will likely either abandon her idea or roll up her sleeves and help—probably the former.

- **Support him.** Too often, a person gets promoted to his level of incompetence. He is in over his head and resorts to low-level management tactics, such as examining the smallest detail or scheduling meaningless meetings with no agenda. He is in the weeds. We should help him. I know it hurts to think about it, but if we help guide the boss's efforts and his communication, and help refocus his time and energy, he will become an ally, and likely support our initiatives the next time we suggest something.

Learning When to Quit

Your son doesn't like seventh-grade band? Let him quit. Training for that marathon is too hard? Just quit. Feeling frustrated or detached from your work? Quit. It's easy. Tired of not making progress on your writing project? Drop it, lose it, let it go. Yeah! That felt good.

When it comes to jobs, there can be plenty of valid reasons to quit, including toxic cultures and lack of professional growth.

But remember: when we quit something, we have to live with

quitting, so we should have a pretty good reason. While quitting might feel thrilling and easy, it's hard to go back—not impossible, but pretty hard. I once heard a story about a rich guy who kept giving so much money to his alma mater that the school named the football stadium after him. Why did he keep giving so much money? When he was a junior at the university, he quit the football team because practice was too hard. He has regretted it for more than thirty years, and he literally kept paying for that missed opportunity.

It's also important to distinguish the difference between quitting and taking a break. Since 2000, I have started a marathon-training plan almost every year. I've only made it to the starting line twice over the past fourteen years, but I always start the plan. Last year my wife and I got up to eighteen miles and stopped. With the kids' schedules, it was too time-consuming. I had to adjust to changing circumstances.

Or, to take a work example, some of the happiest and most successful people I know have a life strategy in which they intentionally change careers and take sabbaticals in the middle of their jobs. This is not impossible to do—it just takes thoughtful planning.

While I don't think lack of commitment to hard work is a legitimate reason to quit something, there are legitimate reasons, including the following:

• **It's impairing health.** Stress-inducing environments, including work, school, or sports, are intolerable. According to the American Institute of Stress, which lists fifty signs and symptoms of stress-related illness, "numerous emotional and physical disorders" have been linked to stress, including "depression, anxiety, heart attacks, stroke, hypertension, immune system disturbances that increase susceptibility to infections, a host of viral linked disorders ranging from the common cold and herpes to AIDS and certain cancers, and autoimmune diseases like rheumatoid arthritis and multiple sclerosis."[7] And that's just part of the list.

We can try to turn around this toxic environment and be the change we wish to see in the world, but if the toxicity is overwhelming, quitting may be the only reasonable option. Otherwise, we could bring that stress home and infect our family and friends. Our health, and the health of the people we love, is more important than our job.

- **It's a professional dead end.** Unfortunately, it's becoming increasingly common to pigeonhole workers into particular jobs, roles, and responsibilities. Gone are the days, it seems, when someone could work her way up through the mailroom and get job experience throughout the organization—the kind of professional experience that leads to personal and professional growth. The companies with the highest retention and the highest levels of innovation offer their employees the chance to work in a variety of positions in the company. Or, as they say on the soccer field, when we play different positions, we "see all sides of the ball."

- **It's devoid of challenge.** "Quit and stay" is one of the saddest descriptions of employees that I've heard recently. It's applied to people who have emotionally and psychologically checked out yet remain in their jobs, punching a clock—either for the money or the simple inability to conceive of doing anything else.

While quitting may be the only viable option to working in a toxic environment, we should think long and hard before we take that action. We should make sure that it's not just because we find the work challenging, perhaps "too hard." Sometimes it takes that extra pound of grit to get through difficult challenges, but that place where we feel challenged—that spot right on the edge of our capabilities where we have to step up our game—is the place where we are at our most creative and productive. When we feel right on the edge of what we are capable of, that's where we'll learn the most.

CHAPTER 7

Strive for Authenticity

On a scale of one to ten, how true are the following statements about yourself at work?

"I feel out of tune with my coworkers."
"I lack companionship at my work."
"There is no one I can turn to in this organization."
"I feel left out."
"I don't feel like I can talk honestly with anyone in this company."

These were among the questions researchers asked 786 professionals and their bosses to help determine their sense of loneliness in the organizational culture, and then to correlate that result with their current job performance.[1]

Recent studies show that a little more than half of us, at one time or another, experience periods of intense loneliness in our professional lives. Loneliness is not depression, shyness, or poor social skills, and it certainly isn't introversion. It's more a feeling of estrangement, of alienation—a sense of not belonging to a place or a culture. And the implications of having lonely people at work are big. Our sense of belonging on a team has a direct effect on our commitment to a task, sense of role clarity, and collaborative effectiveness.

We may find it a struggle to fit in while remaining true to ourselves—to be authentic—but hiding from who we are can alienate us not only from those we work with but also from ourselves. While teammates, bosses, and the larger society around us may pressure us to conform, often for seemingly good reasons, when we are not true to ourselves we can harm them as well as ourselves in the long run.

To be of the greatest value to ourselves, our teams, our families, and the world at large, we must instead strive to be who we are, share what we feel is the best of us, and manage, rather than conceal, our foibles. Forcing people into conformity has a high cost, as diversity of ideas is one of the greatest catalysts to innovation and a sense of self-worth. While building inclusion in the workplace can be a challenge, some simple actions can move us and others in the right direction, as we explore in this chapter.

Hiding Yourself at Work

When we find ourselves isolated, not fitting in, we're likely to increase our level of what the Deloitte Leadership Center for Inclusion calls "covering."[2] That is, we intentionally conceal parts of who we really are. When we feel lonely at work, we may start to pretend to be someone else. And when we pretend to be someone other than who we are, we start to withdraw emotionally.

Loneliness can not only lead us to withdraw but also can affect our health.[3] Feeling socially isolated is directly linked to increased blood pressure and increased risk of heart disease. Loneliness also negatively affects sleep quality, which affects cognition, which... You get the idea.

Here's an example of what I mean: recently, I was asked to be a guest speaker at an event designed for executives of a big technology company. I wore a black suit. The very next day I spoke at a marketing group event of a Silicon Valley gaming company. Unsure of what to wear, I asked, and was told, "jeans and chucks." And then, like an idiot, I asked, "What are chucks?" After I figured out what chucks were, that's what I wore.[4]

This is a pretty benign example of "appearance covering." We do it all the time when we accept a dinner invitation or go to the beach. We try to wear the right thing to fit in, or maybe just not stand out too much. We practice this kind of social covering so much so that, in the Deloitte study, 82 percent of workers stated that covering for appearance was "somewhat" to "extremely" important for professional advancement.

Dressing to fit in can often make us feel even more committed to the team and the mission. But we also often "cover" other aspects of our authentic identities. We hide not only our political opinions but also truths that deeply define us, such as our cultural histories, sexual orientations, socioeconomic backgrounds, or even our age and any disabilities we might have. The following are comments from participants in the study on covering various aspects of their lives:

- **Family obligations.** "I was coached to not mention family commitments (including day-care pickup, for which I leave half an hour early, but check in remotely at night) in conversations with executive management, because the individual frowns on flexible work arrangements."

- **Socioeconomic background.** "I didn't always volunteer the information that I grew up very poor and that I was the first to go to college. It seemed like I wouldn't be accepted because I always assumed everyone I worked with grew up middle or upper class."

- **Ethnicity.** "I don't want people to define me as an Asian, so I've been hesitant to participate in activities geared toward the Asian community."

- **Physical health.** "I don't associate with cancer groups, because I don't want to draw attention to my medical status, disability, or flexible arrangements. People tend to look at me like I'm dying when they find out I have cancer."[5]

However, as the Deloitte study revealed, when we feel like we can be more authentically ourselves, we care more about our work and hold stronger commitment to our company. When we feel that we cannot express ourselves authentically in identity, we feel inhibited in our ability to give our commitment fully to our work efforts.

As one respondent put it, "If I had the opportunity to do the kind of work I do at another firm with similar compensation, but could be more authentic without limiting my job security or chances for advancement, I'd switch in a heartbeat."

We need to remember that partitioning our lives and identities is a trap. When we segment and partition our lives into work life, home life, sporting life, community-service life, etc., we deny the truth that our greatest strength often comes from integrating all our different and diverse network interactions and ideas into a unified and integrated whole. After all, the etymology of "integrity" is from the Latin *integer,* meaning wholeness, or the unit of one.

Tools for Combatting Isolation

Persistent loneliness often leads to an expectation of negative interactions and increased hostility. If we feel socially isolated at work, we begin to expect that isolation will persist—in other words, loneliness begets loneliness. We have to break the cycle. An important step toward this is recognizing a lonely feeling ("No one understands me" or "I don't belong here") as simply an emotional response to a circumstance, or to an individual. And we also need to recognize that we can choose other responses.

Even if we can't conjure up a charitable thought, we can try instead to see the world from the other person's lens, her point of view. When we work on our empathy, we gain greater emotional fluency, which in turn creates connection.

The Five-to-One Rule

As we escalate our leadership capacities, we need to understand that loneliness in the workplace isn't a private and personal issue; it's an issue of organizational culture. If people around us are emotionally withdrawing, it's not their problem, it's ours, and our company's. Aside from direct and personal intervention, we should use a five-to-one rule: create a team interaction dynamic that builds a five-to-one ratio of positive to negative communication.

And by positive, I don't simply mean saying, "That's great!" Research tells us that supportive questions are even more powerful than supportive assertions.[6] So the next time someone on the team has an idea we feel is valuable, we should ask a deepening question, such as "How did you arrive at that?" or "Who do you think we should talk with next to make this a reality?"

According to the research, negative comments and interactions are so powerful, toxic, and lasting, that it takes roughly five positive interactions to offset a negative one. Or, to put it another way, it's

easier to create a positive work environment by reducing (or elimi-
nating) negative interactions than it is to try to combat the negative
with five times the positive.

Fighting Against Pressure to Be Inauthentic

We often put pressure on ourselves to act in ways inconsistent with
who we truly are, for the sake of others or out of fear of being ostracized. But sometimes it's those around us who, intentionally or not,
and often for apparently good reasons, pressure us to be inauthentic.

When my mom was first diagnosed with cancer a few years ago,
her first impulse was to not tell anyone. She thought maybe people
would see her as vulnerable, frail, or dying. I remember thinking,
"That's nuts!"

But it wasn't crazy. It's a common first reaction to getting such
dire news. Instead, she decided to have a very open battle with lym-
phoma and, thankfully, was successful.

It's quite common for people to conceal parts of their identity for
fear of being stigmatized. At work people often hide their religion,
political values, sexual orientation, health conditions, and maybe
their preference for cross-dressing. People even conceal what might
seem to be quite benign things, such as parental obligations to fetch
a sick child from school or take them to a dentist appointment—all
out of fear of being branded as not professional, not dedicated, or,
most important, not like everyone else at work. It's an effort to get
along, to be part of the group, to fit in.

The fear is that, if our true identities are known, we'll be stigmatized, and possibly ostracized, by people at work. Understand-
ably, no one wants to feel rejected. The interesting thing about
this expectation is that it's completely unfounded, according to a

fascinating study from Yale.[7] In the study, researchers discovered that, overwhelmingly, people believed and expected that concealing parts of their identity that were unique or counter to the prevailing culture would make them feel a higher sense of belonging to the group, and in turn the group would be more welcoming and more inclusive to those who look and act like everyone else.

The study showed that actually the opposite is true: when we conceal parts of our identity that are core truths about what we believe and who we are, we start to retract from homogeneous groups. And when we hide personal truths and socially withdraw from a group, people around us sense it and begin to withdraw from us as well. It's a reinforcing cycle.

Once we start to conceal personal identity traits, it also becomes harder to honestly and genuinely connect with others. The result is that we lose a sense of belonging, which is at the very core of one of today's buzzwords: *engagement.*

If we want to feel like we belong where we work, we need to care more about the work we do. To bring out the best in people, we need a culture that not only allows, but actively encourages, expression of self, of who we are. And the very best bosses and leaders understand this by creating an environment of inclusiveness and acceptance, because those basic fundamentals of inclusiveness, social acceptance, and assuming the best in others are the building blocks for accelerating innovation.

Innovating Through Social Diversity

Innovation can come from many sources, but often it occurs when we diverge from the lines of thought of those around us, from being authentic and following our own ideas—it comes when we diverge from the pack. And, while we may think we are unique, often we are building on the divergent thinking of others who came before us.

Think of some of the most iconic ancient innovations: the wheel, the arrowhead, pottery. In each case some*one* knew how to make such a thing, because he was mentored by someone who was knowledgeable in the craft. Each learned a skill that enabled him to replicate a thing of value, hone his skills, and ideally advance the technology to a higher state—perhaps make the wheel lighter, the pottery more resilient to persistent heat.

But who knows how to craft a camera, or a computer mouse, or a compact fluorescent bulb? Indeed, no one person does. Each of these (and many more) current technological artifacts are concoctions of ideas. A point-and-click camera is (as author Matt Ridley puts it) a confection of ideas—silicon, microchips, plastics, lenses, batteries, various refined metals—all mashed together performing a feat of alchemy that represents a camera as we know it, to take snapshots at our children's birthdays.[8]

Since it's nigh impossible to claim sole credit for an innovation, we're at our best when we recognize the deep contributions of all in the value chain that precedes—and follows—whatever we contribute to. The most innovative leaders know how to harness available technology, envision the potential future, and enlist others into action.

Paying the Cost of Conformity

While conformity may seem the safe and sound way to act and think around others, it has its cost. Imagine you are in a meeting, sitting around a table with seven other people, and the person running the meeting presents everyone with two cards, one for the left hand and one for the right. On the left-hand card is a line. On the right-hand card are three lines of differing lengths. You are asked to pick which line on the right card matches the length of the line on the left card.

The answer is obvious. Any fool can see the right answer. But each person, in turn, around the table picks the wrong line, the wrong answer.

Now it's your turn. What do you do? Do you speak your mind? Speak the truth? It's baffling that these people can't see what you see so obviously. What's wrong with these people? It makes no sense. Why did everyone else obviously choose the wrong answer?

About a third of us would agree with the rest of the group. Against our opinion, against what is so clearly obvious to us, we would reluctantly agree with everyone else's wrong choice. These were the results of a series of psychology experiments conducted in the 1950s by Solomon Asch.[9] In these experiments, naïve (uncoached) participants were placed alongside "confederate" (coached) participants. The confederates were coached to give incorrect answers intentionally at different points in the experiment. While 98 percent of the naïve participants correctly identified the matching lines, nearly 75 percent of them instead went along with the group, choosing the incorrect answers.

When the researchers later asked the naïve participants why they ignored what they knew was the correct answer and instead voted as the others in their group did, many said they feared ridicule from the group.

When we perform tasks or engage in activities because, as part of an organization, we go along with the idea that "we've always done it that way," or because the person with the greatest seniority in the room suggested it, we're acting out of conformity. Conformity can be a great thing—it can enable teams to soar and military groups to function seamlessly and efficiently, and allows decisions to be made faster. It means acting in accordance with social standards and conventions, which can offer safety, convenience, efficiency, and harmony within a society. For example, I'm certainly glad we have accepted communication and behavioral conventions over at air traffic control and at the Nuclear Regulatory Commission.

In fact, researcher Charles Efferson and his colleagues demonstrated that social conformity can present a higher rate of correct decisions and higher performance in specific tasks.[10] Conformity is how we deal with the complexity of life, the tsunami of data and information we are presented with, and the unmitigated fire hose of media we are bombarded with. We look at what other people are paying attention to, looking at, and doing. And we do that. It's much easier to follow social convention than to think for ourselves.

But it is not conformity but rather positive and creative deviance that drives change. On December 1, 1955, in Montgomery, Alabama, Rosa Parks, at age forty-two, refused to obey bus driver James Blake's order that she give up her seat to make room for a white passenger. In her own words, she was "tired of giving in."

We are all vulnerable to conformity and, to stay on the creative edge while truly participating in group decision making, we need to be aware of our vulnerability to it. We need to cultivate healthy skepticism toward our own group, and to be willing to disappoint or surprise people in the name of being true to ourselves and for the sake of innovation. It's the difference between belonging to a group and simply fitting in.

When we feel a strong sense of belonging, we feel enabled to be ourselves, wholly and authentically. That sense of belonging gives us better confidence to think and act authentically.

Forcing Conformity by Using Jargon

If we took a time machine back to the 1990s and visited American corporate culture, in addition to wide ties and blocky cell phones, we would also see the Apple Newton in action and fax machines widely in use. There was the Netscape IPO of 1995, Japan was the king of semiconductors, and the NASDAQ tipped over one thousand points.

We would also find people talking differently. They didn't use the word "business model" widely. That term wouldn't make its way out of MBA classes for a few more years, and people were still largely thought of as resources to be applied against goals, objectives, and strategies. According to Harvard business historian Nancy Koehn, people weren't talking about "energy," "passion," or "purpose" in the way we do today.

Language certainly matters a great deal. The words we use when interacting with one another say a lot about what we believe and value. But I'll argue that repetition and overuse of insider language—or bafflegab—can balloon into an enormous crutch. If we do a Google search on "bafflegab," we find that it's an informal, North American noun meaning "incomprehensible or pretentious language, especially bureaucratic jargon." While playing with jargon can be fun—it's the reason why the online game Business Buzzword Bingo exists—its use can undermine authenticity and lead to disaster, especially when we are forced to conform to its use.

According to the *Los Angeles Times*, in the 1980s Pacific Bell publicly abandoned a failed $40 million "leadership development" effort based on the work of Charles Krone, former aspiring mystic turned management consultant.[11] The training program attempted to get everyone in the organization to adopt new, and often fantastical, language to gain efficiency and speed.

During this expensive and failed experiment of confusion and lost productivity, "task cycle" was an invented term used to describe a system of managing a problem. Even the word "interaction" had its own, impenetrable, thirty-nine-word definition that employees had to understand.

Pushing people to speak and interact all the same way, as Pacific Bell did, is the equivalent of enforcing a mental dress code.

There are plenty of annoying popular business phrases out there. "Let's not try to boil the ocean" means let's not waste time on something that will take forever. Rowing to Australia would take a long time, too, but we don't say that. Incidentally, the expression "boil the ocean" supposedly came from the humorist Will Rogers when he was asked how we should deal with German U-Boats during WWI. His answer was to simply boil the ocean, and he added that the details of how to do that are up to someone else.

And how did "out of pocket" come to mean unavailable? This phrase has several other meanings, including a financial one—reimbursable expense, as in the cost came "out of my pocket." But, although I searched and searched, I found no satisfactory explanation for how it also came to mean unavailable. One source does say that this usage dates back to the early 1600s, although the *Oxford English Dictionary* found the earliest specific reference to it in a 1908 O. Henry story, "Buried Treasure."[12]

"Over the wall" needs to be canned, too. It means to send something, like a document or a proposal, to a client or a vendor. But, metaphorically, it's alienating. The expression suggests we're dealing with someone foreign, even hostile. Why does it need to be a wall?

"Low-hanging fruit" came out of the 1980s restructuring at General Electric. Peter Drucker had been hired by Jack Welch in the early 1980s to help get GE out of a down-cycle (damn, I did it myself!), and they worked together to try to remove corporate jargon from the conversation. Ironically, along the way they created more new terms in an attempt to destroy the old language. In addition to "low-hanging fruit," that exercise also brought us the terms "rattlers" (meaning obvious problems) and "pythons" (meaning bloated bureaucracy).

"Burning platform" conjures images of Gandalf and the Balrog fighting over a crumbling bridge above a cauldron of fire. We should stop conjuring, and just use the simple, well-understood, time-honored word "urgent" instead.

The list goes on and on. Let's keep this one: "ducks in a row." I like it. It's cute. It comes from the days before bowling alleys were automated, when humans had to place the bowling pins upright.

Whatever the common bafflegab in our organization, we should simplify our language. If an expression replaces one that is simpler and more familiar, and needs explanation to anyone outside our company, we should avoid using it.

Learning to Build Inclusion

Instead of conspiring to make everyone speak a special language as an act of conformity and to avoid hearing diverse voices, the authentic way to build teamwork is to work on building inclusion by embracing diversity.

On the playground at my daughter's elementary school, at recess, there is something called the Buddy Bench. According to Annie, it's where you can go and sit if you don't have any friends to play with.

If you see someone sitting there, alone on the Buddy Bench, your job is to go over and invite the kid to play with you.

My first reaction to the thought of the Buddy Bench was that it sounded a bit like the No Friends Bench, that the act of sitting

there was sad and lonely, and that walking over and inviting someone to play was an act of generosity and kindness. I thought that the
whole scene of walking over and sitting there would be like social
abandonment.

If you did have the courage to walk over, in front of the world,
and take the hand of someone sitting on it and invite her to play
with you, the two of you would be quietly ostracized as you played
in a corner of the playground. At least that's the way it played out in
my mind. Maybe I've watched too many come-from-behind, under-
dog Disney movies.

But the way my daughter describes it, so matter-of-factly, there's
nothing odd or strange or uncomfortable about either going to the
bench to sit, or walking over and inviting someone sitting there to
play with you. By sitting on the Buddy Bench, she explains, it's almost
as if you are announcing that you are available to play. It seems the
gesture of sitting there is more of an invitation. It's like raising your
hand and saying, "Hey, I'm free for something new. Anyone?"

There doesn't seem to be any stigma associated with it. It's all
very straightforward. If you're not sure what to do, sit on the Buddy
Bench and pretty soon someone will come over and invite you to
play. Annie says people don't sit on the Buddy Bench for very long.
Almost immediately kids get scooped off it by some kid or a group
of kids, and run off immersed in an activity.

To me, this represents the epitome of environments of inclusion—
an environment in which no one is permitted to be a pariah. The
school has created a mechanism by which, if you feel lonely, lost, or
simply unsure of what to do next, you make a gesture. That gesture of
sitting on the bench says to the entire community you are feeling left
out or simply disengaged, and the whole community sees this visual
cue and reacts immediately.

It's also a culture in which a call for help has no stigma associated with it. In fact, the inverse is true. Regular rotation through the Buddy Bench is perfectly normal and healthy, since that kid is going to get picked up by a new group and have new experiences.

But unwritten social rules say it is unacceptable for anyone to remain on the Buddy Bench for long. I imagine that someone's lingering on the bench would be an unconscious cue that the community lacks leadership, or courage. The social contract would be broken if someone were left there hanging. Annie says it never happens.

If we're concerned about someone's lack of engagement, or professional isolation, in our work environment, we should be proactive about it. We can start by assuming that this person is at the company for a reason—that he deserves to be there. Then we need to recognize the cues: lack of contribution at meetings, unanswered e-mails, missed deadlines, lack of initiative, low dedication to work. We should then pick up the phone, or walk over to his cube, and invite him. Invite him for coffee. Invite his opinion. Invite him to contribute to our most valued project. Invite him to play.

Giving Credit and Accountability

If we really want inclusion and to promote authenticity, we must also share the credit for successes while making everyone accountable for her actions.

Paul Hiltz, the president of Springfield Regional Medical Center, whom I first introduced in chapter 2, might be one of the toughest interviews I've had, but for reasons you might not expect.

It's not because he isn't articulate. He is widely praised for his ability to clearly communicate a compelling vision of the future. His mind is sharp. His ideas are clear. His voice is calm and reassuring.

It's not because he's too busy to talk to me. He answers all of his e-mail personally and promptly, and gave me his personal cell phone number and encouraged me to call with any questions. I called him once without a scheduled meeting, and, after we said hello, he asked me if I had a couple of minutes to talk.

It's not because he conceals key parts of his business that he can't share. Not at all. Hiltz is known as constantly initiating projects of transparency, and building education campaigns to ensure that everyone clearly understands how the business works. He once hired financial consultants to conduct workshops to teach everyone how the healthcare business works.

And it's not because he is inaccessible, tied up in the boardroom or in meetings. Quite the opposite, Hiltz spends almost all of his time in the hallways, having lunch with patients, or meeting families of patients. The staff describe him as being constantly visible both in the hospital and in the greater community.

The real reason Hiltz is such a tough interview is because most of the time, when I ask how he led a big process reinvention, or developed a remarkable financial turnaround, or constructed an entirely new service rollout in the hospital, he tells me I should talk to this department head, or that nursing administrator, or the other communications director. Every time he tells me it was really the other person's doing, saying, "She took the lead on that" or "He made it happen; talk to him."

So I talk with the people Hiltz points me to, and they all tell me the same thing: yes, they were part of the equation, part of the team, but they all point back to Hiltz. It's Hiltz's leadership, they say. They say everyone in the hospital is simply rallying around his clear vision of a comprehensive, high-quality healthcare environment— a healthcare system fully integrated with the greater community. Everyone understands the goal, and everyone is committed to the mission. One of the doctors in the hospital system described Paul as "a healing leader"—a leader who is able to heal wounds of distrust, to heal the lacerations of broken communication.

Welcome to a new style of open leadership—a leadership style that believes in flipping the approach to leading:

- Using influence, not coercion
- Focusing on collaboration instead of individual heroism
- Treating employees the way we want customers to be treated
- Instilling continuous, not episodic, habits of learning
- Giving, not taking, credit
- Assuming accountability, but also giving autonomy
- Building inclusive, not homogeneous, cultures

Paul Hiltz represents the epitome of an effective leader in the twenty-first century. He guides rather than directs, influences rather than commands, and encourages rather than threatens. He has managed to galvanize the entire organization around a higher goal by constantly giving credit, and the spotlight, to someone else.

By constantly giving credit where credit is due, Hiltz is also giving accountability. Accountability, if accepted and embraced, requires us to become fully present and focused to achieve excellence. For true excellence, quality of work, and quality of relationship, we must be wholly present and mindful. As we will explore next, before we can take action, we need to be mindfully aware of our circumstances and relationships.

CHAPTER 8

Be Fully Present

While leadership sometimes requires action, it sometimes means simply showing up and being fully present.

Being fully present means listening intently, being aware of ourselves in each moment, and being aware of our colleagues' moods and dispositions. It also means focusing on the task at hand, ignoring distractions. Focusing on that task not only helps get the work done but also sends a message that the conversation is important, and that relationships with our colleagues are important. And when we're fully engaged in our work, we also know the limits of what can be done and when our team is on the wrong track.

In this chapter we explore the concept of being fully present and, closely associated, the state of mindfulness, and how being fully present and mindful affects the quality of our relationship with others. We also discuss how our actions are visible reflections of our beliefs, and how our actions are also statements to those around us. We spend some time understanding that distractions undermine the quality and attentiveness we give to our work, and explore some of the ways we can mitigate those distractions. Finally, we take time to recognize that, by applying empathy and patience to mindful efforts, we can often achieve extraordinary, and surprising, results.

Being Fully Present Through Mindfulness

The definition of "mindfulness," a concept with Buddhist roots, varies depending on the source. The *Merriam-Webster Dictionary* defines it as "the practice of maintaining a nonjudgmental state of heightened or complete awareness of one's thoughts, emotions, or experiences on a moment-to-moment basis."[1]

Mindfulness is also about relationships. In fact, as Dr. Richard Chambers and Margie Ulbrick write in their book *Mindful Relationships: Creating Genuine Connection with Ourselves and Others*, "mindfulness *is* relationship"—with ourselves and the world around us, our environments, and the people we interact with. It's about how we experience our bodies and our emotions, and each other.[2]

Sitting with a loved one, or alone, watching and enjoying a sunset is a mindful moment. Walking our dog in the park, or preparing a meal, or listening to music can all be mindful experiences, if we are fully present, focused, and undistracted. At work, we can be mindful, sitting quietly in a meeting and listening thoughtfully to the ideas and opinions of a colleague, if we are undistracted and listening with unbiased openness.

Mindfulness is accessible to everyone. It's not a mystical, elusive experience, and it's not necessarily meditation, but rather an intentional therapeutic technique that has value for all of us in our increasingly hectic everyday lives. We are always racing from here to there—racing in our relationships, and racing in our work. For decades people have attempted to do everything faster, even reading faster in vain attempts to absorb information faster.

But a growing body of new evidence suggests that the path to heightened comprehension and immersive learning is by reading *slower*, not faster. The same is true for taking notes in a meeting or in a classroom. Computers have allowed us to type pretty much everything we hear verbatim, but doing this does not allow us to process and internalize the information in the same way as when we take notes longhand.

Writing ideas down old-school style with pen and paper slows us down, forcing us to distill ideas into notes that have meaning to us. Therefore, in the moment of listening, we are also synthesizing the ideas into characters and images that make sense to us, deepening our understanding and comprehension. By slowing down our note taking—processing and reiterating information in real time—on the page, in our own style, we are practicing a form of mindfulness.

In a series of experiments that demonstrated this phenomenon, researchers asked separate groups to take notes verbatim on a laptop (group 1) or handwritten on paper (group 2). Consistently the pen-and-paper note takers beat the laptop note takers in recall exercises one week later.[3]

Slowing down, focusing, and becoming increasingly mindful and fully present is an important element in elevating our presence and effectiveness. As Scott Eblin, best-selling author of *Overworked and Overwhelmed*, likes to say, "Leadership presence requires being present."[4]

The fact that greater comprehension and content cognition comes from slowing down makes perfect sense when we understand that, at a fundamental level, mindfulness is—in the words of Ellen Langer, one of the world's foremost scholars on mindfulness—"the process of actively noticing new things."[5] It makes sense because to notice new things we must be present, open, and aware.

Mindfulness isn't a tiring exertion. When practiced thoughtfully, it's a relaxing and absorbing activity that makes us feel renewed and energized. Mindfulness is about being able to integrate various disparate parts of our lives into a unified whole. Remember, the word "integrity" comes from the Latin *integer*, meaning wholeness or one.

This integrated, holistic notion of mindfulness dispels the antiquated philosophies of work–life balance, as if these were two separate lives that needed to be in harmony. Instead, mindfulness teaches us to understand our lives as one integrated whole.

Stress is not a function of an event itself—it's merely our emotional reaction to it, a function of the *perspective* we take. The event itself is impersonal—neither positive nor negative. When we apply mindfulness, we begin to understand that, instead of simply reacting to events, we can *respond* to them in a more meaningful way.

For example, let's say our team has a big product launch and in the first quarter that product bombs. No one buys it. If our team views that as purely a negative event, everything involved in it becomes seen as bad—the product, our team's performance, etc. But if we can step back and impartially examine all the circumstances of the event—for example, the market dynamics, customer buying habits, product placement, or interface design—we can mindfully explore, and then change, the situation to create a more desired outcome.

Being Aware of Our Actions

"Every decision is a statement," says Hap Klopp, founder of The North Face. "Some are statements to the masses. Some are statements to the few. But all are statements to and about yourself."[6]

I've been learning a lot from Klopp lately. I interviewed him in San Francisco in April 2015. Since then I've reread his 2012 book, *Conquering the North Face: An Adventure in Leadership*, and his new book, *Almost*.

The latest lesson I've been reflecting on is that, from the perspective of everyone on the team, the boss's actions are extremely visible, and hyper-analyzed. Lowland gorillas, who share 98 percent of our DNA, look at their troop leaders every fifteen to twenty seconds for cues of how to behave—when it's time to move on and forage, when it's time to be alert and focused, and when it's time to chill out. Our primate cousins are not that much different from us in looking to the leader for social cues.

Early in his career, Klopp was hired to help turn around a ski shop. There were many things wrong—the inventory, the accounting, the customer service, even the simple layout of the shop in terms of making equipment visible and accessible. The most critical things that needed correcting were the accounting and the vendor-sourcing practices, which entailed calling vendors to speed up the company's delivery. But that contribution wouldn't be the most visible to employees, so instead he focused his energy on working with the warehouse employees to clean, reorganize, and restructure the company's entire warehouse.

Klopp's standing up on a ladder reorganizing the warehouse with the team didn't make the biggest dent in the bottom line immediately, but it did send a very clear and obvious message about work ethic, collaboration, and leading by example. By showing up in a very real, visible way and focusing on the task at hand, Klopp was making a small act of leadership that had great ripple effects.

Later, when The North Face was taking off rapidly, it would move into bigger office spaces every six to twelve months. The company developed the custom of having a painting party every time it took over a new space. Klopp would join these painting workdays not only to demonstrate his willingness to work side by side with everyone in the company but also to get to know people.

Every leader I've encountered who is described by peers and colleagues as "exceptional" or "remarkable" or "excellent" lives his or her work life (and often personal life as well) in a highly visible manner. Such leaders are not locked in the boardroom, or hiding in their offices, but are front and center, readily available and open to ideas. It's a small and simple act that can have a big impact.

Being Fully Present in Our Work

Being fully present, especially with all the mobile devices we have these days, is not always easy. As we explore in more detail in chapter 12, distractions of modern life, especially mobile devices and technologies, can have a big effect on our interactions with others, undermining our relationships and work.

Just how distracted are we, and how big an impact can that have on our lives? In 2009, *Car and Driver* magazine wanted to figure out how dangerous texting and driving can be, compared with drunk driving.[7] They rented an 11,800-foot airport runway in the middle of Michigan and put Jordan (twenty-two years old) and Eddie (thirty-seven) behind the wheel.

They rigged up a red light in the middle of the windshield to represent brake lights in front of the driver. A passenger had a little remote control to activate the light randomly and measure the drivers' response times. They tested the drivers at both 35 mph and 70 mph. The average reaction time while the driver was sober and paying attention was 0.54 seconds to start braking. Now they had a sober baseline.

Then they asked the drivers to pick up their smartphones and read funny quotes from the movie *Caddyshack* and then text funny quotes from the movie while driving. Reaction times varied, of course, but both drivers performed worse than when they were undistracted. Some were considerably worse.

Then they took a break and chilled out on the tarmac to get a good buzz on. They mixed up some vodka and orange juice and drank away an hour or so, until the drivers blew a 0.08 on the Breathalyzer. Then they repeated the test. For the most part, the younger driver Jordan, outperformed the older driver, Eddie but not always, as shown in the results.

At 35 mph:

- Reading *Caddyshack* quotes—added up to forty-five feet before the driver reacts
- Texting *Caddyshack* quotes—added up to forty-one feet before the driver reacts
- Intoxicated—added up to seven feet before the driver reacts

At 70 mph:

- Reading *Caddyshack* quotes—added up to thirty-six feet before the driver reacts
- Texting *Caddyshack* quotes—added up to seventy feet before the driver reacts
- Intoxicated—added up to eleven feet before the driver reacts

That's right. Intoxication is not even close when it comes to the distractions our devices offer. Reading or texting on your smartphone is *way* more impairing than driving drunk. The *Car and Driver* experiment puts it up to six times more dangerous.

Driving is second nature to most of us. It just requires paying attention and following the traffic rules. Obviously, texting impairs our ability to do that. But how does texting affect our work? Active listening, mental processing, creative engagement, and problem solving all require much higher cognitive and collaborative participation. So, when we are texting and e-mailing while in meetings or on conference calls, what's our impairment level? Twenty times greater? Thirty times? And how does this translate into impact on our work? We should ask ourselves, "What's the business opportunity loss when the people in my company are constantly distracted?"

It's not news to anyone that multitasking is debilitating in many ways. The simple action of switching from one task to another is, in itself, a cognitive drain. Not only that, simply *attempting* to multitask lowers our IQ performance to that of nearly an eight-year-old, according to a study at Stanford University.[8]

To be fully functioning adult leaders, we need to be truly present. And to be truly present, we need to shut down the smartphone and fully engage in the task, or conversation, at hand. When we engage fully in the moment, sometimes remarkable things can happen...

Showing Up with Empathy and Understanding

From the kitchen window, actor Christopher Reeve could see that his wife, Dana, was getting frustrated. Over and over again, she was running awkwardly, hunched over, down the driveway while holding onto the back of Will's bicycle. Their son Will, six years old at the time, was still terrified of riding without his training wheels, or without his mom holding him up. Reeve watched as his wife and son repeated the same failed routine again. Finally, Dana came inside, exhausted and frustrated.

Reeve said to his wife, "Let me try." He rolled his wheelchair gently down the ramp outside and onto the driveway, where his son was wiping away tears. Reeve spoke to his son slowly. Since the accident, Reeve's voice had become soft and measured. He told Will to place both hands on the handlebars and hold them steady. He explained that, by doing this, the bike wouldn't shake as much. He told Will to look up, far ahead, to where he was going and not down at the pedals or the front wheel. He told his son to first place his right foot on the pedal and his left foot on the ground, prepared and poised to push hard.

Will froze. Then Reeve reminded his son that he would never let him do anything too scary or dangerous—that riding a bike was something he knew Will could do. He told Will he was going to count to three, and on three, it was time to go. Reeve counted slowly, and, when he reached three, Will pushed off hard and rode down and around the driveway. The first time he circled back, his face was a mask of concentration and focus, and the second time around his face only reflected joy.

In his book *Nothing Is Impossible*, Christopher Reeve writes that, before the accident that left him paralyzed, he was a whirlwind of activity.[9] He constantly took his family sailing, horseback riding, traveling, hiking, and adventuring around the world. He writes that he never really asked if they wanted to go; he just took them. And after the accident, he learned to listen. He learned to speak to them where they were, trying to see their perspective, with a deep sense of empathy.

Reeve writes that, before his accident, he would not have believed that he could teach his son to ride a bike simply by talking to him. Teaching, he had thought, was about showing, demonstrating, and physically leading the way. But during his recovery process, he learned the power of conversations, words, intentions, and meeting people at an intersection where they are ready to learn. He learned this because the physicians and caretakers around him would introduce an idea or an activity, but only when they thought he was ready to tackle it, or else he would push it aside. It's all about introducing learning opportunities when people are ready to learn.

An important nuance of excellent leaders is that they have the capacity to recognize when others are ready to go to the next level—ready to take on a new challenge—and, instead of doing it for them, encourage their heart and prepare them to make that leap. A small act of leadership starts by simply showing up and being willing to share your skills and experience.

Showing Others It's Okay to Let Go

Following procedures can be a good thing. Having clear protocol bolsters confidence and spurs clear, intentional action. Captain Chesley B. "Sully" Sullenberger maintained something pilots call "deliberate calm" in the face of his emergency water landing on the Hudson River on January 15, 2009, when the Airbus he was piloting lost both engines after flying through a flock of geese. As highly experienced pilots will describe, that landing was not as miraculous and untenable as many believe. Sully was simply following standard procedure when he calmly glided the Airbus to a water landing.[10]

In that example, Captain Sully thankfully held on with "deliberate calm" to his training and experience. But sometimes we hold on to ideas or possessions when it's really time to let go.

In 1994, fourteen heroic firefighters perished in the South Canyon fire in Colorado. According to the Wildland Fire Leadership Development Program, although the firefighters had been instructed to drop their gear when fleeing the advancing fire, none did.[11] One body was found only 250 feet from the safety of the top of the ridge, still wearing his heavy pack and carrying a chainsaw.

After the event, experts calculated that, if the firefighters had run just a half-mile-per-hour faster, they would have outrun the fire. Average humans, unencumbered, can run about twelve to fourteen miles per hour for short distances. Carrying their gear might have cut the firefighters' speed by half. Perhaps they were disoriented in the smoke and fire. Perhaps the act of dropping gear would be to admit failure. Perhaps in the moment, and in spite of their training, they didn't hear the order and simply never thought of it.

We consistently overvalue our possessions. In the 1949 wildfire disaster at Mann Gulch, crew foreman Wag Dodge clearly ordered everyone to drop their gear and run from the advancing fire. Walter Rumsey testified that, even though he was running for his life, he saw that his partner, Eldon Diettert, was carrying a shovel. Rumsey grabbed it from him to lessen his load, but then searched around for a tree so that he could carefully lean the shovel against it.[12]

In moments of intense pressure, we can get caught up in our foolish consistencies and adherence to habit in the face of changing circumstances, which keeps us from being fully present. In both wildfire disaster examples, the firefighters simply couldn't see that the circumstances had elevated to the next level—that, in fact, protocol dictated that it was time to drop everything and run.

We can also become so enamored with our possessions, physical or mental, that we self-identify with carrying them, to the point that we refuse to let go, even when it's time. To carry a Pulaski fireman's axe, invented by a famous firefighter and inventor Edward Pulaski,[13] is a badge of honor, just as carrying our habits and opinions with us everywhere we go affirms who we are.

We not only tend to overvalue our physical possessions but also our decisions. How can we identify those fixations that are holding us back and weighing us down, while reaffirming those closely held convictions that empower and propel us? Taking a tip from Harvard medical researcher Jenny Rudolph,[14] I suggest that the best advice is to say what we are thinking out loud, in the presence of those whom we trust and who will hold us accountable.

In her research, Rudolph found that, once medical students

made incorrect diagnoses, they would often persist in ineffective treatments long after it had become obvious that the treatments were not helping. They were simply unable, or unwilling, to revisit their original diagnosis. They became stuck—fixated—on their original decision. Instead they should have tried the following steps:

- Say out loud an expanded list of the symptoms identified
- Say out loud an expanded list of the possible diagnoses that would fit the symptoms identified
- Say out loud a plan to eliminate each diagnosis one by one

By simply saying out loud what we are thinking in the face of changing circumstances and evidence, we force ourselves to consider our opinions and biases, and to be fully present in addressing the task at hand, to be mindful instead of focusing on previous decisions we've made. We not only hold ourselves more accountable but we implicitly ask those around us to check our judgment.

Showing up each day with mindfulness and presence, and modeling the behavior you believe in, is a small act of leadership.

CHAPTER 9

Inspire Others

When I was a teenager, I worked at a greenhouse and had a boss who gave vague instructions, such as, "Go water the plants." That's pretty nonspecific in a nursery that covers five acres. So I would disappear and water plants for several hours, never knowing how much water to give, or which plants required more or less water. In addition to the lack of direction, I found the whole thing pretty boring. I lasted about six weeks before I quit. I never questioned what I was doing or why. Inspired I was not.

The previous chapters describe ways to build great teams and lead them, but the one component that every great leader needs is inspiration, as we explore in this chapter.

One of the greatest predictors of effectiveness, happiness, and success in work is our capacity to inspire others. As Canadian researchers Val Kinjerski and Berna J. Skrypnek found in studying the effect of inspiration in the workplace, "Inspired leadership emerged as central to influencing individual experiences of spirit at work." It was also "strongly linked" to a sturdy organizational foundation, organizational integrity, a positive workplace culture and space, a sense of community among members, opportunities for personal fulfillment, continuous learning and development, and appreciation and regard for employees and their contribution.[1]

Inspiration is rooted in passion, in curiosity, and in our desire to live our lives to the fullest. To inspire, we must *be inspired*, and to be inspired, we have to take time to notice the small acts of leadership readily available in any situation.

There's nothing quite so inspiring as seeing someone embrace his work in the pursuit of excellence, or in service of a greater mission. There's nothing quite so moving as witnessing small acts of excellence, generosity, and kindness. Often the most moving and inspiring stories are about competitors who become comrades or everyday people taking deep pride in their work.

For example, there's the beautiful story of high school runner Meghan Vogel, who helped her fallen competitor, Arden McMath, cross the finish line of the 2012 Ohio State Track meet.[2] Or the following story of quiet dedication and inspiration that Martin Seligman recounts in his book *Authentic Happiness*.[3]

Embracing Your Life's Calling

Psychologist Martin Seligman was visiting a dear friend in the hospital. His friend, Bob Miller, at the age of eighty-one, was still a vibrant, joyful man. Gregarious and an avid runner and tennis player, Miller had been hit by a truck while running, and now lay in a coma in a hospital bed for the third day.

The neurologist gently asked Seligman to look at Miller's do-not-resuscitate order and consider removing the life support system. Seligman was distraught as he considered the possibility that his friend would never rise again. He asked for a moment of quiet, the doctor left the room, and Seligman sat down in a chair to watch the orderly working.

The orderly was quietly rearranging art on the walls. He took down a calendar, pinned up a Monet print, and took two Winslow Homer prints from his bag and placed them with consideration on the walls. Next to Miller's bedside, the orderly taped a photograph of a Peace rose.

Seligman gently asked the orderly what he was doing, and the man replied that his job was being the orderly on the floor, but he brings in new art prints and photos every week. The orderly explained why: "You see, I'm responsible for the health of all these patients. Take Mr. Miller here. He hasn't woken up since they brought him in here. But when he does, I want to make sure he sees beautiful things right away."

In his memorable "Street Sweeper" speech, Martin Luther King Jr. also extolled the values of embracing our work: "If a man is called to be a street sweeper, he should sweep streets even as Michelangelo painted, or Beethoven composed music, or Shakespeare wrote poetry.... If you can't be the sun, be a star. It isn't by size that you win or you fail. Be the best at whatever you are."[4]

Some people have jobs, some have careers, and some have callings. Jobs are a means to another end, such as supporting family leisure time. Careers are driven not only by money but also by professional advancement. Often, when advancement stalls, alienation and disengagement set in. As we learned earlier from the Ernst & Young study, in chapter 3, professional advancement ranks among the most important motivators for professionals.

Yet a calling is a pursuit of something greater than oneself, and this is the path to the highest inspiration for others, as epitomized by a story Peter Drucker tells about a Nurse Bryan in his classic book *The Effective Executive*.[5] This nurse elevated the level of care and excellence by constantly asking the simple question, "Are we doing the best we can to help this patient?"

Nurse Bryan was not a supervisor, or a leader with a title, yet the patients under her care consistently recovered faster than patients on other floors. Her words became a mantra, known as "Nurse Bryan's rule," spreading throughout the hospital system, from doctors to orderlies, with remarkable results. According to Drucker, her creed had permeated the culture and lived on more than a decade after Nurse Bryan retired.

Nurse Bryan's small act of leadership was to consistently give not only her attention but also her time to her work, and to her patients.

Giving the Gift of Time

Everyone is so busy these days, overwhelmed by complexity and uncertainty, that it's hard to know what to do or who to talk to in order to accomplish initiatives at work that are daring and unexpectedly awesome. And so we create structure, process, and teams to solve specific tasks or projects. But team composition, proximity, and facilitation matter a great deal in terms of how productive they eventually become.

Some of the very characteristics that define modern professional teams are the same characteristics that undermine their success, including the following:

- **Diversity.** Assembling teams that are technology enabled, globally dispersed, and diverse is a rapidly growing trend and with good reason, because the ability to leverage expertise throughout the globe is increasingly a powerful component of competitive advantage. But deeply engaged, open collaboration starts with trust. And trust starts with the personal understanding that comes from cultural and emotional fluency. We might get technically proficient collaboration across cultural boundaries, but richer collaboration requires the bedrock of trust.

• **Size**. Teams are swelling in size to be (or appear to be) more inclusive, gain greater stakeholder buy-in, and leverage more expertise. Teams of twenty or more people are increasingly common, and technology is enabling a swelling head count. "My rule of thumb is that no work team should have membership in the double digits," says J. Richard Hackman, formerly of Harvard University, who spent his career studying teams, "and my preferred size is six."[6]

• **Education.** Teams are increasingly made up of people with higher and higher education levels. And, it turns out, the higher the education among the team members, the more likely the team may devolve into petty arguments. One key to overcoming this obstacle is to require teams to have not only task goals but also relationship-oriented goals.

To boost effectiveness and ingenuity of teams, as well as to eradicate "fault lines" within teams, leaders can do one thing that has a powerful effect in scaling excellence: give the gift of time.

Leaders' regularly giving their time to listen to emerging problems and advise team members about whom they might talk to within the company to accelerate solutions, and to just listen to team members' aspirations for the work they do, is a defining characteristic of successful cultures in organizations.

Mentoring programs, in which employees (often new hires) are paired with an experienced employee, increase retention rates, as researcher Nicole Frost and her colleagues found: "By incorporating leadership initiatives such as inspirational motivation, individualized consideration, idealized influence, and intellectual stimulation, nurses and leaders can use mentoring to improve professionalism, confidence, and self-worth."[7]

The upshot is that those who are mentored are likely to stay longer in their role. And it's not just nurses who benefit from such mentoring, according to Jonah Rockoff, who studied the relationship between mentoring and retention in teachers: "My most consistent findings are that teachers whose mentor had prior experience working in their school were more likely to return to teaching in their schools."[8]

Whether we are in education or healthcare or a corporate environment, when we, as leaders, make the small act of giving our time to others in a mentoring or tutoring role, they feel inspired, enthused, and energized. One of the most powerful behaviors of effective mentors, as with all leaders, is an ability to listen intently, without bias or interruption.

Truly Listening

We never know from whom the next big idea will come, but we're unlikely to hear it if we aren't listening. And truly listening to those around us, no matter who they are, is not as easy as it may sound. Truly listening means not only opening our minds to what others have to say but giving people the time to fully express their thoughts, to express what inspires them and what they aspire to.

Years ago, a young professor at the University of Virginia, James Pennebaker, conducted a series of experiments with his new classes. In his book *Opening Up: The Healing Power of Expressing Emotions*, he explained that he would divide them up into groups for just fifteen minutes and ask them to talk about anything they liked.[9] These groups were composed of students who didn't know one another, so they talked about their hometowns, how they got to the university, what they were studying, and so on.

After the group broke up, Pennebaker would ask them to estimate how much talking each person did in the group, how much they enjoyed their group, and how much they learned from others in the group. Consistently, those who did most of the talking claimed to have learned the most, and liked their peers the most. It seemed that the more they talked, the happier they were about the people around them. In fact, as Pennebaker repeated the experiment, he discovered that the larger the group, the greater the effect and the more the biggest talker liked the group. The effect diminished as the group got smaller, to the point that, in a one-to-one conversation, if one person dominated the conversation, both people reported disliking it.

Energizing Others

Slydial is the app that lets you go straight to voice mail, safe from the possibility that someone might actually answer your call. Slydial exists in part because of the energy vampires in the world—those people you dread talking to because they leave you depleted, bummed out, frustrated, or annoyed with every conversation. However hopeful you remain, they will figure out how to suck the energy from the conversation. Sure, maybe you use Slydial because you just don't have the time for a conversation and a text would get lost in translation, but I don't think that's the biggest reason it's so popular.

Being an energy vampire is antithetical to being a source of inspiration. To avoid being an energy vampire, we should ask ourselves, "When people leave an interaction with me, do they leave feeling more or less energized?"

How important is being able to energize those around us?

According to Rob Cross, associate professor at the University of Virginia's McIntire School of Commerce, our ability to create energy in the workplace, with our colleagues around us, is a more powerful predictor of our success than other criteria, including function, title, department, expertise, seniority, knowledge, and intelligence.[10] These are all descriptors. Creating energy is a behavior, and it can be learned. The ability to generate energy in those around us is so important that many successful executives and leaders place it at the top of the list as the most important attribute in team members.

Inspiring others by energizing them doesn't have to do with backslapping or pumping people up with platitudes or grandiose conference-room speeches. We can all become energizers by developing the characteristics energizers have in common:

• **They are fully present.** Creating energy does not require that you be extroverted. We don't need to jump up and down, or stand on a chair and cheer, or high-five our colleagues. As we explored in the previous chapter, it simply means that we possess the ability to see opportunities as others describe them and reiterate those ideas in a way that conveys true understanding.

• **They open up possibilities.** Energizers possess the ability to ask provocative questions that open up possibilities and encourage pursuit of action. It means being present and engaged in each conversation. It means building contagious enthusiasm in a constructive way, with emotional fluency. Opening up possibilities is about giving those around us the creative latitude to explore ideas that perhaps fall outside of usual organizational boundaries.

• **They follow through.** Getting enthusiastic about something can be infectious. But enthusiasm and action are different.

There's nothing more de-energizing than walking away from a project meeting feeling fired up, thinking we're working diligently on a shared vision, only to return to working on the project and find our colleagues haven't done anything on it. That's a case of unrequited inspiration. Energizers follow through on their promises and consistently demonstrate that a project can be done by actively contributing.

- **They add value instead of trying to top others.** I'm sure you have been in a meeting before in which an idea is tossed around, and each person in turn tries to outdo the others to look smarter. This is not adding value but rather "topping" someone else—trying to sound smarter and more important than the other person is and competing with her instead of contributing to the conversation. So when someone says, "We went to New York for our vacation," and then you say, "Oh, we went to Spain," that's not building value. That's trying to top someone else's contribution.

- **They use supportive questions.** Sometimes we can fall into the conversational trap in which we tend to lead the conversation toward our own interests, ideas, and concerns, what Charles Derber, a professor of sociology at Boston College, calls "conversational narcissism."[11] Someone says his child is playing the trombone, and the narcissist says, "Oh, I used to play the trombone. Let me tell you about it." And off you go for half an hour, lost in memories of middle school band.

To leave a conversation with both ourselves and other people energized, enthused, and even provoked, we should instead use what Derber refers to as supportive assertions and questions. A supportive assertion could be an evaluation, such as "That's awesome!" or a comment, such as "You should check out this article on that." But the supportive *question* is even better. It shows active, interested engagement in the conversation. A supportive question encourages and deepens the conversation. Through such supportive questions, we lead the other person into sharing more of her experience, ideas, and passions.

• **They share their vitality.** We all know that feeling when we are not only inspired but at the top of our game, feeling alive, passionate, and excited. "Employees who experience vitality spark energy in themselves and others," Gretchen Spreitzer, Christine Porath, and their colleagues found, and "companies generate vitality by giving people the sense that what they do on a daily basis makes a difference."[12]

Telling Real-Life Stories

Sue Mahony, president of Lilly Oncology, is responsible for almost two thousand people. In an interview, she described to me some of the ways she found to inspire her team:

• **Avoid suggestions becoming orders**, or your team is unlikely to provide honest feedback.

• **Lead with questions**, composing questions that rely on the strength of the team members and enable their expertise to shine, such as "What would happen if we made this decision?" or "What are the technical considerations if we build this?"

• **Conduct listening sessions**, in which her only goal is to find out what people around her honestly think, care about, and prioritize, after which she thanks them.

- **Get closer to the impact of the work**, to be able to judge better how team members are doing.

The last behavior is pretty easy to get team members excited about and driven in their work, considering their goal is to save lives, but it's also easy to build petty squabbles and get exhausted in dealing with the mundane. This is why Mahony works to regularly remind people of why they are there. Real-life people currently suffering, and recovering, from different forms of cancer specific to the team's work are brought in to tell their story. And their story is not always about the nature of the disease itself but also about the human side. When the researchers on Mahony's team hear about the human impact, they are united in their sense of purpose and focus—the stories inspire them.

Hiring the Right People

I had an interview in November 2015 with Victor Cho. He is currently the CEO of Evite, the digital invitation service. You may have used the service to organize a dinner event or your kid's birthday party. Evite currently has about seventy employees, which, as Cho describes it, is big enough to offer a full spectrum of organizational challenges, yet small enough to remain nimble in this volatile technology market.

When it comes to hiring and placing the right people in the right roles at Evite, Cho considers three primary criteria:

- **Skills and capabilities.** Do candidates have the skills and capabilities to do the job, and are they willing to constantly learn and gain new capabilities? As he described, it's certainly important that people arrive with great skills for whatever role they are applying for, but, more important, he believes, is a constant willingness to learn, grow, and develop new capabilities along the way. This is the growth mindset we discussed earlier.

- **Points on the board.** How much are candidates contributing to organizational goals? It's something Cho refers to as "points on the board." That is, how many hard, measurable contributions are people making toward the company's vision. This could be measured in lines of code, or sales made, or product improvements.

- **Energy accretion.** Cho describes "energy accretion" as one's ability to build a positive sense of curiosity, enthusiasm, and can-do attitude on the team. It's how much people in the organization contribute to and accelerate the positive energy of those around them. If "points on the board" is the science of evaluating performance, then "energy accretion" is the art of evaluation. Cho views this subjective, and hard-to-quantify, trait as more important than short-term contribution or raw skills.

Cho has the least patience with those who disrupt the chemistry in the organization by draining the energy from it. He is more forgiving and patient about the first two factors—skills and capabilities. He knows skills can be learned and developed. And points on the board can be coached, and often can be influenced by external factors.

Bad chemistry and negative mojo can quickly spoil the energy of an entire team. In Cho's opinion, this is where many leaders can often get sidetracked, holding measurable contributions in highest esteem. It's an easy trap to fall into. After all, if we want results, who cares how the work gets done, right?

But thinking this way is a mistake. When we start to reward results by any means, at any cost, we celebrate lone heroes and place individuals above the team. Our focus should be on inspiring teams to come together and work toward common goals, creating an environment where we all prosper. As we explore next, teams, when properly aligned, have the power to create something we alone cannot.

CHAPTER 10

Clarify Roles

History is littered with disasters that came about because the wrong person was in charge at the wrong time, or because who should be in charge was unclear. Sometimes these disasters occurred through miscommunication, and sometimes because leaders neglected their roles.

The key to a beautifully crafted machine is that every part works, and is in the right place—in the role it fits. The same is true of teams in the workplace.

Team rituals can help clarify and reinforce team roles, and we can tell by just looking at the interactions among team members how well they will work together. As leaders, our role is not only to lead but to be the glue that holds the team together. When leaders put their teams first, and have their back, team members feel freer to challenge the status quo and innovate.

Aligning Roles with Information

On the morning of July 3, 1988, the crew of the USS *Vincennes* was particularly edgy. Early in the morning hours, one of the *Vincennes* helicopters had been deployed to investigate some boats trafficking in their area of the Persian Gulf.

The helicopter pilot reported receiving small-arms fire from the boats. The *Vincennes* was stationed in Iranian waters and captained by Captain William Rogers. Rogers retaliated by firing upon the small vessels, which heightened the tension in the darkened Combat Information Center, a small war room inside the *Vincennes* that was lit up with control panels and computer screens. Much of modern warfare is staring at computer screens.

The Ticonderoga-class guided-missile cruiser had been hastily deployed from San Diego, California, only a month earlier and rushed to the Persian Gulf to increase security. It had also been outfitted with the new, state-of-the-art Aegis surveillance system. (More on that later.)

Meanwhile, at 10:17 a.m., Iran Air Flight 655, a civilian Airbus carrying 290 passengers and crew, took off from Bandar Abbas Airport for a twenty-five-minute flight across the Strait of Hormuz to land in Dubai. Many of the civilians on board were making a sacred journey to Mecca.

Shortly thereafter, tacticians on board the *Vincennes* started tracking Flight 655 as it approached their location. At that moment, the sophisticated Aegis surveillance system provided a critical piece of misinformation. Even though the airliner was accurately broadcasting an identifier as Mode III, or civilian, the system falsely identified the Airbus as instead Mode II, a military combat F-14, a plane more than two-thirds smaller.

The second error was human. A tactician monitoring the plane's approach toward them incorrectly stated that the plane was descending toward the *Vincennes*, possibly as an act of aggression, when in fact the plane was ascending to a cruising altitude of fourteen thousand feet. Strangely, the fancy system was not designed to provide information on changes in altitude, so, to compute altitude changes of aircraft being monitored, operators had to compare altitude data taken at different times and make the calculation on their own, manually, on scratch pads, or on a calculator—and all this potentially during live combat.

Rogers radioed the captain of the nearby friendly frigate USS *Sides*, Robert Hattan, and asked him to confirm what they identified as an approaching F-14. Captain Hattan disagreed with the Aegis's assessment. All operators and monitoring systems on board the *Sides* correctly identified the airplane as a commercial jet ascending, not descending, in a standard commercial flight path.

Rogers listened to the conflicting identification coming from the *Sides* and decided that the superior technology and monitoring system of the Aegis outclassed the information from the frigate. The fancy Aegis technology gave Rogers a superior sense of confidence and the willingness to disregard Hattan's warning.

At 10:24 a.m., Rogers ordered two missiles to be deployed. One hit the airliner, which killed all 290 passengers on board. The *Sides* and crew were later awarded a Meritorious Commendation for "outstanding service, heroic deeds, or valorous actions," in part for their efforts to dissuade Rogers from launching the attack.

This tragic incident involved many mitigating factors—human, technological, and situational. Following the incident, lengthy congressional hearings and investigations were held.

From this recounting of the story, it's clear that a primary cause of the disaster was a lack of clear team member roles.[1] Team performance and team decision making can often be flawed, particularly under pressure situations, if roles are not clear. Had the two crews built redundancies or decision-making processes to question or confirm the information from different angles, the disaster might have been avoided.

It's trendy and cool to talk about flattening companies, destroying hierarchies, and that large-scale "holacracy" experiment going on over at Zappos. The definition of holacracy, according to the website holacracy.org, is "a new way of running an organization that removes power from a management hierarchy and distributes it across clear roles, which can then be executed autonomously, without a micromanaging boss."[2] But here's the thing: whatever the team or project situation we're trying to solve, role clarity is critical. Not every situation requires a "boss," but we do need a decision-making process, and we need a balance of expert roles on each team.

This is true on soccer teams and on high-performing expert teams, such as media crews or emergency-response teams. And it's certainly true of those ad hoc innovation teams that come together in a company to be the "voice of the customer" or whatever the company calls it.

When I interviewed Tammy Erickson, author and adjunct professor of organizational behavior at London Business School, in September 2012, she said role clarity in team environments was often the most overlooked characteristic in building high-performing teams. Often the team, or the boss, makes the assumption that, if they put super-talented people together, they will change the world.

They will, but only if they know who is supposed to do what.

Putting the Right Person in the Right Role

Next time you're standing at the gate waiting to get on a flight, watch when the crew shows up. Watch how they interact with one another. Do they laugh? Do they ask questions they don't know the answer to? Does it sound like they are listening well to one another? Or do they ask questions out loud—to no one in particular—and answer themselves?

They are all pros, and they work at the same airline, but there's a very good chance they have never met one another. Yet, it turns out that how these professionals interact in the first few minutes will tell you a lot about how effective they are going to be shortly as a team up in the sky.

Mary Waller, a researcher at York University in Toronto, has been studying something she and her colleagues call "swift-starting expert teams."[3] These teams are everywhere—TV news crews, emergency-response teams, event organizers. They are composed of highly specialized professionals who assemble for a specific job or task and often have little or no previous interaction with one another, but do share the following characteristics:

- Are competent and familiar with complex work environments
- Work quickly under situations of time pressure
- Have a stable role on the team but ad hoc team membership
- Have complex, interdependent tasks that rely on interactions with teammates

It turns out that how members interact with one another during just the first fifteen to twenty minutes is highly predictive of how they will perform as a team for the entire duration of the job. The reason is that interaction patterns established early in these relationships usually persist throughout them, on any operation in which they serve together.

Waller and her colleagues tracked each piece of dialogue team members uttered and identified the patterns in which they develop. For example, "Input the coordinates" is a command. "We have good weather today" is an observation. "Maybe we should ask tower control" is a suggestion, and "What should our heading be?" is an inquiry. The researchers categorized each segment of their communication as disagreement, humor, anger, small talk, observation, agreement, question, and more. They found the communications within well-performing teams to have the following characteristics:

- **They are simple and consistent.** The researchers discovered that patterns of interaction often emerged quickly and persisted throughout the relationship. And the highest-performing teams established patterns that were simple, consistent, reciprocal, and balanced with one another. The lowest-performing teams had a greater variety of conversational patterns, more unique communication patterns, and members who showed a lack of reliance on other team members.

- **They are short and targeted.** While big locker-room pep talks or command-center speeches look good on television, they aren't terribly effective in driving team excellence. The most effective teams kept their communication short, precise, and targeted to a specific task or job sequence.

- **They are balanced.** In the study, the researchers measured what they called "reciprocity," that is, to what extent the team members relied on one another and balanced participation in communication. For example, if a team member showed "mono-actor" behavior of asking and answering her own questions, it demonstrated that she showed less reliance, and less reciprocity on other team members.

Here's an interesting twist in the study: the researchers hypothesized that any mono-acting behavior would be on the part of the pilot currently in control. They thought that the person with command of the airplane would be the one offering the least reciprocity.

But that was not the case. It was the PNF (pilot not flying), who lacked control of the plane, who exhibited the greatest amount of mono-acting behavior—in other words, was least likely to act as a team player.

The truth is that most of us are professionals with expertise in our own areas. Most of us have jobs that are specialized and specific to our own unique talents. And that trend is continuing. Increasingly, organizations are hiring specialists, and job tenure is shortening—meaning we are all working more and more in swift-starting expert teams.

If we keep our team communications consistent, targeted, and balanced, our teams will soar. Team rituals—however small or humble—will help us better define who is doing what on our teams.

Defining Roles Through Small Team Rituals

In our house, if the coffee isn't ready by the time my wife leaves to teach, her mojo is off for the whole morning. I'm sure lack of caffeine is part of the problem, but it's only half of the story. Another meaningful part of the process is the brewing of the coffee, the pouring of the coffee, the stirring half-and-half into her favorite mug, in just the right quantity, and sipping the coffee on the drive to school. The *ritual* of the coffee is as valuable as the taste and the caffeine.

Rituals performed in groups can be even more powerful. When we take time as a team to savor moments or engage in rituals before events, we can greatly affect the outcomes. For example, simply taking time to share a toast before a sip of wine will make the wine taste better to everyone. The principal reason is that the ritual forces everyone to be present in the moment. Another form of savoring is when we close our eyes while listening to music we enjoy. By intentionally closing one sense, we are opening and accentuating another.

These are small examples of savoring experiences, which involve taking time to appreciate and amplify the small moments of life such that they become more powerful and meaningful. Families are the most basic and essential teams in our lives. And building positive rituals in our families can have immense impact.

"Additional research found that children who enjoy family meals have larger vocabularies, better manners, healthier diets, and higher self-esteem," author Bruce Feiler writes. "The amount of time children spent eating meals at home was the single biggest predictor of better academic achievement and fewer behavioral problems."[4]

Sports teams innately understand the power of rituals. Consider the awesome and fear-inducing haka performed by the New Zealand All Blacks rugby team before every game. This powerful expression of native dance not only reinforces their heritage and cohesiveness as a team, but also channels any pregame anxiety into unified energy and focus. In this instance, the haka ritual also acts as a social glue to bind the team together.

We can easily build rituals into the culture of our business teams as well—for example, around the way weekly and monthly team meetings are handled. These meetings often involve the same people, and the more junior participants usually speak less while the boss speaks more, which is exactly opposite to what a healthy culture looks like. Healthy, participative teams want ideas and insight from everyone at the table.

Paolo Guenzi, in his book *Leading Teams*, offered an idea for how to change this team ritual for the better: tell everyone in advance of the meeting that, if they don't participate and share their best ideas, they could get a yellow card as a warning.[5] Two warnings will win them a red card, which means they aren't permitted to attend the meeting next week. We don't need to be too worried that people will intentionally get a red card to leave the meeting. It's not likely people will actively seek negative reinforcement to get themselves kicked out.

We need to remember that we engage in these small acts of leadership to build better, more functional teams because our teams allow us to accomplish things that we cannot do alone.

Putting the Support Team First

Rona Cant, of Oxford, England, should change her name to Rona Can. In an interview in late 2014, Rona said that, after being an English housewife and raising two children in the 1990s, she decided something was missing from her life. She wasn't the type to host afternoon tea, so she started a business in fabrics and upholstery. That wasn't quite satisfying enough, so she decided she needed another degree and enrolled at a university. Something was still not quite right. She felt a bit unfulfilled, so she started taking sailing lessons.

Finally realizing she was confusing busyness with fulfillment, she signed on to a yacht crew to race around the world. But before she could feel competent to race, she completed the arduous Yachtmaster ocean certificate to ensure her capability and contribution on the boat. She also completed a course in diesel-engine mastery, just in case the ship's engines needed repair while far from harbor.

Then she participated in another around-the-world yacht race, then a third race around Great Britain and Ireland—and this time she won. Now you know the kind of flinty, tenacious, can-do person that Rona is. But what does this have to do with clarifying roles and how we interact with our teams? Her early adventures gave her the experience and knowledge to apply small acts of leadership in her next audacious adventure.

After winning the sailing race around Great Britain and Ireland, Rona signed on to be part of a three-person expedition to drive dog-sleds five hundred kilometers (three hundred miles) through the remote wilderness and mountains of Norway. They drove the dog-sleds to the very tip of the Norwegian landmass, where it touches the Arctic Ocean, to a remote outpost of snow and ice on the edge of the world called Nordkapp. It wasn't even a trail. In fact, the goal was to create the trail, to pioneer it, so that the trip could be done again.[6]

During my interview with Rona in 2014, she described something I found fascinating about dogsledding in the northern wilderness and that stressed how important clear roles and teamwork count in such a potentially dangerous situation. Each evening the dogsledders would camp near a frozen lake or river. While her traveling partner, Cathy, erected the tents and Rona built a fire and untethered the twenty-eight sled dogs and inspected them for cuts and injuries, their guide, Per Thore, would take an immense auger and drill a hole through as much as a meter of ice to create a well from which to retrieve fresh water. Rona would then hike to the well, post-holing her way through the waist-deep snow, to ladle forty liters of water into a plastic container and haul it to the campsite.

Several trips were required to deliver all of the water to the spot where Thore was busy sawing chunks of frozen reindeer meat to mix with dry food and the water, which he'd then set over a camp-fire to make a stew for the dogs. The dogs required more than sixty kilos of food per day.

And then Rona would return to the hole in the ice to retrieve ten liters of water for the humans. You see, only after the dogs were fed and cared for would the humans take their first sip of water. When you hear her tell the story, the reason is obvious: without the dogs in the wilderness, you die. Without the dogs, you are going nowhere. They are the engine that makes the expedition possible, and without their health and well-being, and rest and focus, all is lost.

The people on our teams, in our organizations, are the reason our companies exist at all. And when bosses spend all their time working, refining, and advancing their own agendas—their own missions and aspirations for promotion, money, or recognition—it's the beginning of the end. Things start to break down, and not just the processes and the integrity and quality of what the company delivers. The very people within the organization begin to suffer emotionally and even physiologically.[7]

Remember, we need to nourish our people first. The only difference between ordinary and extraordinary is the decisions we make—when we put our teams first, our expeditions, and our work, will go great places.

CHAPTER 11

Defy Convention

The term "deviance" has long been associated with behavior that is harmful, dangerous, or perhaps immoral, such as lying, cheating, stealing, and other dishonorable acts. But sometimes bucking the norm in a positive way—positive deviance—may be more honorable behavior.

"Positive deviance focuses on those extreme cases of excellence when organizations and their members break free from the constraints of norms to conduct honorable behaviors," writes professor Gretchen Spreitzer of the University of Michigan. "It has profound effects on the individuals and organizations that partake and benefit from such activities."[1]

Positive deviance is the kind of behavior that, when recognized by others, should be commended and praised. It refers to actions that, although outside and even disruptive of the norm, have honorable intentions and positive outcomes.

In this chapter, we look at what happens when bad behavior becomes the norm and how people who deviate in a positive way can drive positive change. As we've learned throughout this book, rising to the capacity of great leadership and impact can start with small acts, small changes in behavior. Not only leaders with power and influence but anyone, at any level, can act to start the change—from a lone arborist saving trees or a doctor combatting infection in a hospital to leaders of large organizations.

Slipping into Unethical Behavior

"The culture of any organization is shaped by the worst behavior the leader is willing to tolerate," educators Steve Gruenert and Todd Whitaker wrote in their book *School Culture Rewired.*[2]

In the news today, as I write this, the fallout from the Volkswagen fiasco has reached global proportions. If somehow you haven't heard, it's been called the "diesel dupe." As a BBC News article explains, Volkswagen was found to have installed a device that defeated emissions testing, effectively changing the performance results of the emissions tests on its diesel vehicles.[3] This "defeat device" was actually a piece of software designed to recognize when the vehicle was undergoing emissions testing by detecting test circumstances. VW has admitted to installing this device on eleven million cars worldwide.

Beyond the mechanics of the deceit and the politics of the scandal lies the question, "How could the people and the culture within Volkswagen have permitted this?" The device was too integrated and sophisticated to have been a mistake produced by lack of oversight, confusion, or even ineptitude. The device, and the deceit, had to be carefully engineered and intentional. But were the engineers working on the software truly aware that they were committing an unethical act?

Diane Vaughan is a social scientist who coined the term "normalization of deviance" to describe the way organizational cultures can begin to drift morally and rationalize that drift over such a slow time horizon that they aren't even aware of it themselves. Rather than being positive, this kind of deviance is destructive.

As she wrote about in her book *The Challenger Launch Decision*, Vaughan studied the infamous 1986 *Challenger* space shuttle explosion and discovered that faulty O-rings, linked to the disaster, were identified as fallible long before the disaster occurred.[4]

NASA, from the beginning of the space shuttle program, assumed that risk could not be eliminated, according to Vaughan, because the ability of the shuttle to perform in a real launch could only be mathematically predicted and tested in simulations. For that reason, the engineers expected anomalies on every mission, and disregarding danger signals, rather than trying to correct any problems, became the norm. For example, after space shuttle *Discovery* launched on January 24, 1985, and then returned safely to Earth, engineers performed an autopsy on the vehicle, which included carefully examining the O-rings.

In disassembling *Discovery*'s O-rings, the engineers discovered an alarming amount of grease that was blackened from exceedingly high pressure and temperature. The O-rings in the *Discovery* launch held but were more damaged than they had been in previous launches. Engineers calculated that the O-ring temperature at the time of *Discovery* liftoff was approximately 58 degrees Fahrenheit.

"[*Challenger*] could exhibit the same behavior," the engineers reported after the examination. "Condition is not desirable, but is acceptable."[5] They also recommended proceeding with the next launch of *Challenger*. In fact, they not only recommended proceeding with the next launch, engineers painstakingly argued their position regarding the tolerable O-ring damage in a formal report.

At the eleventh hour, only a day before the fatal launch, engineers Bob Ebeling[6] and Roger Boisjoly[7] contradicted themselves and strenuously argued to NASA officials that the O-rings could stiffen and fail to properly seal the joints of the booster rockets because of the cold January temperatures. These arguments were not persuasive to NASA officials because, after all, they had the original detailed engineering report stating that the risk was acceptable.

It's important to understand that the engineers were not simply acting or pretending that the damage was acceptable. Up until the engineers made their final plea to officials to halt the launch of *Challenger* only the day before, they actually believed that there was nothing wrong at all with that classification.

"No fundamental decision was made at NASA to do evil," Vaughan wrote. "Rather, a series of seemingly harmless decisions were made that incrementally moved the space agency toward a catastrophic outcome." The O-ring damage observed after each launch *was* normal. The culture had simply drifted to a state in which that condition was also considered acceptable.

In the NASA example, the existence of the damaged O-rings after each launch was deemed acceptable. It became an implicit, and accepted, rule that everyone simply tolerated and believed to be quite normal. But if we step back for a moment and study the situation, as Vaughan did in her analysis, that acceptance of damaged O-rings seems pretty crazy.

Questioning the Craziest Rules

Last year I heard the most amazing behavioral science story. It goes like this: several years ago researchers working with monkeys confined five in a single enclosure. Each day they placed a banana at the top of a ladder. The monkey who first climbed and attempted to retrieve the banana was sprayed with cold water. And then the rest of the monkeys were also sprayed with cold water. Miserable.

After a few days, the monkeys started grabbing, holding, and biting the monkey who attempted to get the banana, because of course everyone else would get doused with cold water. Pretty soon no one attempted to get the banana. They learned that they would get both sprayed with cold water and attacked by their peers if they tried to climb the ladder—two miserable outcomes.

Then one day the researchers removed one of the monkeys and brought in a new monkey. The very next day the new monkey raced to get the banana but was immediately set upon and attacked by the other monkeys, who refused to allow him to reach the banana. The new money is likely thinking to himself, "What the heck? What's wrong with you monkeys?"

After several days of repeatedly being held back, finally the new monkey succumbed to the culture and stopped trying to reach the banana each day.

Over time the researchers would remove one of the older, experienced monkeys and introduce a new one. And each time the new monkey was taught by his peers not to go for the banana. Until finally, all of the original monkeys had been rotated out and only newer monkeys, trained by their peers, remained in the cage.

And still no monkey attempted to get the banana each day, although no monkey now in the cage had ever had the experience of being doused with cold water. While no monkey in the enclosure could ever explain or understand *why* none of them tried to get the banana, they all complied with this "rule" that had no logical origin.

The story is amazing, a poignant metaphor for our everyday lives. Immediately I started looking for the original study to read it, and write about it. It has fascinating implications for our personal lives, our teams, our workplaces, and our inability to question why we participate in the habits and rituals we do every day without even questioning them.

Here's the thing: the story isn't true. According to Dario Mae-stripieri, a professor of comparative human development, evolution-ary biology, and neurobiology at the University of Chicago, the experiment never existed; the study never happened.[8] It was origi-nally described in a business book twenty years ago and repeated over and over by many others. I was disappointed but not surprised. The story is so plausible and compelling that it begs to be told.

Like the monkeys in the banana story, we can easily get trapped into repetitive behaviors without ever asking why we do what we do. And, as with the banana story itself, we sometimes find stories so compelling that they become folklore, repeated over and over until they become gospel truth without anyone ever questioning the origin.

Often we believe that, if we try something new—attempt a novel experiment at work to improve a process or develop a new product—our bosses and peers will meet us with rejection. So we stop trying. But we should still show up every day with an open mind and willing to try something new—go out on a limb, smash a barrier, break a taboo.

Organizations need to constantly guard against slipping into a norm that is unproductive and even potentially dangerous, and be on the lookout for, and embrace, deviance that is positive.

Embracing Positive Deviance

The concept of positive deviance first appeared in nutrition research in the 1970s, when researchers Monique and Jerry Sternin observed that, despite the poverty in a community in Vietnam, some poor families had well-nourished children even though they did not have access to additional money or resources. The researchers used the information gathered from these outliers to plan nutrition programs, drastically reducing the rates of youth malnutrition.

"It's easier to act your way into a new way of thinking, than to think your way into a new way of acting," the Sternins and coauthor Richard Pascale subsequently wrote in *The Power of Positive Deviance*," which they based on their research.[9]

Fortunately, some people choose to go against the flow of behavior around them, yielding positive results. Such was the case of Paul King, a British arborist, and Jon Lloyd, an American doctor.

Saving Trees

The Arbor Day Foundation describes the elm tree as "stately with its vase-shaped, broad crown...a tree whose history is closely linked to much of American history."[10] But in the twentieth century, elms came under attack by a fungus. The fungus caused what became known as "Dutch elm disease." The disease, first identified in 1921, was spread by elm-bark beetles and had wiped out elm trees around the world, from Asia to Europe, and finally in the Americas. By the early 1990s, very few mature elm trees were left in the United Kingdom.

Over the years, experts had tried many different interventions to stop the spread of the disease.[11] Early efforts focused on cutting down diseased elms or burning them, in attempts to isolate the problem. Later arborists tried using chemicals, such as DDT, but stopped after they discovered the DDT not only killed the beetles infecting the trees but also endangered birds, squirrels, and pretty much all organisms, including humans.

In the 1970s, treatment of Dutch elm disease switched to biological fungicide weapons, which have been largely, and often completely, ineffective. Finally, the University of Amsterdam developed a vaccine in the 1980s that has been more effective than previous efforts.

Paul King tried something completely different. During the 1980s he was working in Essex, England, as an arborist. His job was to go around the countryside and trim bushes and trees. He was always amazed and impressed by two elm trees near his home that somehow were thriving while, elsewhere throughout the country, elms were sickened with disease.

"My job in the 1970s and 1980s was cutting down diseased elms," King is quoted as saying in an article in the British newspaper *The Independent.* "Over the years we must have cut down thousands and it was heartbreaking. But I always noticed how these two particular elms near my house somehow survived."[12]

As the article goes on to explain, King decided to try an experiment. In the 1980s, he took cuttings from the two healthy trees and from those cultivated more in a greenhouse. Over a period of thirty years, elm trees across the British countryside continued to be decimated by Dutch elm disease, with the notable exception of those cultivated from King's original cuttings.

Scientists are not quite certain what makes King's strain of elm so resistant to Dutch elm disease, according to the article, and it's possible his trees may succumb over time. But, at the moment, he was creating a novel, and positively deviant, solution to a persistent and systemic problem that was previously unsolvable.

Solving a Widespread Infection Problem

Darryl was a wounded war veteran at the Pittsburgh VA hospital back in 2005. While in the hospital, he acquired a nasty bacterial infection, Methicillin-resistant *Staphylococcus aureus* (MRSA), which required four separate surgeries on the wound on his leg.

Of the various incidental bacterial infections we can get inside a hospital, MRSA is one of the nastiest. The symptoms are swollen, painful red bumps that resemble pimples or boils. The affected area might be warm to the touch. And unlike, for example, the AIDS virus, which is fragile and easily perishes in open environments outside the host, MRSA can live on hospital surfaces for up to six weeks. Between 1976 and 2004, hospital-acquired MRSA infections increased thirty-two-fold. The Centers for Disease Control and Prevention estimates that each year almost two million people get an infection simply from being in a hospital. Those hospital-acquired infections kill almost a hundred thousand people each year as well.[13]

Darryl knew that he'd gotten the bacterial infection either through direct contact with someone carrying the bacteria, or by contacting a surface or medical device that was carrying it. When doctors, nurses, and clinicians walked into Darryl's room, he watched them closely. If they didn't wash their hands, he smiled warmly at them and then looked at the sink. If the medical providers didn't get the gesture immediately, he did it again until they got the point. It was patients like Darryl who prompted the hospital to post signs in the rooms that say, "You have a RIGHT to clean hands. Please remind EVERYONE to sanitize or wash their hands when entering and exiting your room."[14]

Doctors Jon Lloyd and Rajiv Jain led the MRSA prevention efforts for the VA Pittsburgh Healthcare System. They had previously tried a top-down, mandated approach to preventing the spread of the bacteria. On the basis of the continuous improvement principles of the Toyota Production System, the hospital had begun making cleaning agents and gowns readily available for the clinicians and instituting a mindset of "hand hygiene."

The approach worked, but it was also slow and expensive because it required purchasing expensive supplies and materials and hiring additional staffing to monitor and administer the program throughout the hospital system.

Then, in 2005, Lloyd read an article in *Fast Company* magazine about positive deviance and the research of Monique and Jerry Sternin in Vietnam. He was intrigued and, following the Sternins' model, he and the medical caregivers at Pittsburgh's VA hospital looked around the facility and found people, such as Darryl, who were successfully implementing their own small deviant practices, with incredibly positive results.

Lloyd had a eureka moment. "The expertise to tackle MRSA is right under our noses," he declared. "There are hundreds of experts here. The key is recognizing that the solutions to the problems exist among the staff and the patients." Thereafter, Lloyd and Jain began to collect the positive-deviance practices of clinicians and patients, then share and teach those practices until they became formalized and part of the social fabric of the hospital community.

Since 2009, the incidence of healthcare-associated infections has been decreasing steadily in the United States, in part because many healthcare organizations across the country have adopted the practices pioneered by Lloyd and Jain.[15]

Reaping Financial Rewards Through Positive Deviance

On Monday, August 29, 2005, Hurricane Katrina made its third and most devastating landfall, with sustained winds of more than 125 mph. Inside the headquarters of Hancock Bank in Gulfport, Mississippi, Katrina's thirty-foot storm surge had driven four feet of water throughout the ground floor and destroyed the elevator system.

A tornado had ripped out thirteen thousand windows on the face of the building and blown glass, furniture, and debris throughout the interior. The bank had a one-inch-thick steel roof that had been peeled off by the gale-force winds, exposing the interior of the seventeen-story building to the storm and deluge. And in the basement, the central data center was being flooded and blasted with falling Sheetrock as the interior walls crumbled and fell.

As reported by James Pat Smith, of the Gulfport Community and Regional Resilience Institute, COO John Hairston, in the shelter of a nearby building, managed to call security IT manager Jeff Andrews, who was in Chicago.

"Jeff, the building's a total loss," John yelled into his cell phone as the winds howled outside. "You've got four days. Bring up the systems, get it current. I may not be able to talk to you again for a while.... If we cannot get the systems up, we don't have a company."[16]

The following morning, the bank executives huddled over the hood of a car in the parking lot. It was Tuesday, August 30. The next day would be payday. Most of their customers would be getting paid the following morning, many by direct deposit. They needed those funds desperately for basic food, shelter, and clothing. Credit cards would be useless. The region was devastated, the infrastructure flattened. With sporadic electricity available, cash would be critical to sustaining people's lives.

Serving customers from Texas to Florida, Hancock Bank was one of the primary banking providers in the region. But without power at its branches or ATM facilities, there was no way the bank's customers could access their funds to buy basic needs. Fifty of Hancock's regional bank branches were offline, with no power or access to customer account information.

Those executives in the parking lot of Hancock's headquarters then did something remarkable: reminded of the original charter of the bank to serve communities first, profits second, they asked their branch managers to open no matter what. Without power or lights, and some without doors or windows, that afternoon ten locations opened for business. Several of those locations served customers from card tables in front of the shattered bank. Within three days, thirty locations opened for business and invited people in.

In exchange for an IOU on a Post-it Note, with only a name and an address if they had no identification, each makeshift bank provided $200 in cash to anyone who asked for it. That's right—in the critical week following Katrina, without requiring either proof of identification or verification of account information, Hancock Bank pulled cash from destroyed ATM machines, dried it out, and put $42 million into the local economy.

According to bank CEO George Schloegel, less than $200,000 was not returned. And in the five months following the disaster, thirteen thousand new accounts were opened, and bank deposits grew by $1.5 billion. Yes, billion. Hancock Bank had definitively become the bank of the community.

That's the power of knowing the right thing to do and actually doing it, no matter how far it deviates from business as usual. It's what happens when leaders are courageous enough to disrupt the status quo, deviate from the norm in a positive way, and live their values—just as the CEO of Schering-Plough did in the next story.

Encouraging Others to Be Positively Deviant

At a global company meeting in October 2003, in Atlanta, the new CEO of Schering-Plough, Fred Hassan, stood onstage before thousands of sales professionals from around the world and said the following: "If you are put in a position where you must decide between making a sale that involves doing something you don't feel comfortable with—something you won't be proud of later—and walking away from that sale, then walk away. As your CEO I'm telling you to choose long-term trust and integrity over short-term gain."[17]

Hassan had only been named CEO in April of that same year. His philosophies and opinions were not yet well-known throughout the organization. He knew he was taking the risk of alienating some of the successful sales professionals who were making a killing on quarterly commission checks from short-term transactions. In addition to providing this message of focusing on integrity, he led the change of the commission structure to incentivize longer-term relationships with customers. He knew some salespeople would leave, and they did.

But something else happened. Starting in the spring of 2004, Schering-Plough enjoyed more than four years of double-digit growth. Then came 2008, and the growth ran dry for most everyone. Yet, even during this period, Schering-Plough continued to innovate and introduce new pharmaceuticals to the market, as well as to return consistent earnings for shareholders and community. Schering-Plough hired and retained those sales types who took the long view.

In a conversation I had with Hassan in April 2013, he put it this way: "People want to do something right and be a part of something bigger than themselves. . . . I didn't expect it, but I got a long standing ovation that day."

In this example, Hassan refused to accept the dogma of the past, instead deviating from the norm in a positive way, rejecting the common philosophy of "that's the way we've always done it around here." That phrase, when adopted as a mantra, can be the greatest impediment to progress and innovation. Like the executives at Hancock Bank, Hassan was deeply courageous and willing to lead with the strength of his values and conviction. He was, in effect, asking the entire sales force to upend the way they do business to align with higher values.

Most organizations include individuals or groups whose uncommon practices or strategies enable them to find better solutions to difficult or intractable problems. The trick is to find and identify these positive deviants and collect their stories and practices, and then scale them. Any of us can play the role of disrupter. And any of us can harness our curiosity and find those positive disrupters who live in our midst. It just takes a little courage and curiosity.

CHAPTER 12

Take a Break

We've learned a lot and come a long way in this book. In our work to commit constantly to small acts of intentional and incremental leadership behavior, we may overlook a seemingly small act that can reap huge benefits—taking a break.

Hitting the pause button can help us gain a new perspective, refresh our creative energy, relate better to our team members, and spur innovation. While this may be a small act, it's not always easy. We get used to the paths we take day after day, which often lead to comfortable ruts in our personal and professional lives, and intentionally breaking that pattern can be difficult but rewarding.

Despite new technology intended to make our work easier, professionals around the world are working longer hours. The small steps toward changing dead-end and stressful behaviors made over time, such as intentionally taking breaks, can not only make us feel more energetic and optimistic but can also positively affect relationships with those around us.

As we explore in this final chapter, how we spend our days is how we spend our lives. If we learn to take breaks, our lives are likely to be longer, healthier, and more productive. Taking breaks not only refreshes our thinking but also calms us, so that we can deal with difficult or unexpected circumstances, seeing such events as learning opportunities rather than potential disasters.

In our desire to step up to challenging tasks and complete them, we often trade rest for bingeing on work—staying up all night, whether to prove to our bosses or teams we can do it or because management demands it. Research shows that, far from being beneficial, pulling an all-nighter can be less fruitful than taking a break. Such all-nighters can even be dangerous, as when the *Exxon Valdez* tanker spilled oil off the coast of Alaska, after a sleep-deprived third mate was left at the helm.

Sometimes it's not our bosses but our devices that seem to be ruling us, depriving us of the break we need to find an innovative approach to a thorny challenge, build better relationships, or just ponder the universe, which has led to some of the biggest innovations. Constant interruption can fragment our thoughts and our lives, and a steady flow of information from our computers, smartphones, and other electronic devices just becomes noise from which it is hard to extract valuable input. Sometimes the most productive thing we can do is take a break from all our electronic devices— put them down, disconnect, walk away, and give ourselves time to think.

We may think we're too busy to take a break, but research shows that temporarily walking away from difficult tasks or the daily grind is often more productive and can lead to better solutions more quickly. The busier we are, *the more we need a break.*

With all the stresses of modern life, we should mindfully choose not to succumb but instead choose to be happy, as we explore in the next section.

Choosing Happiness

Does the following sound like you?

You rush around in the morning, get yourself ready, get the kids off to school, and hustle through traffic to get to work on time. You commute twenty to forty minutes every day. You have your own cube, but it feels like assigned seating. There is stark fluorescent lighting overhead. You attend at least two meetings a day (sometimes more), neither of which you needed to attend, and during these meetings there is endless discussion of minute issues that could have been resolved in twenty minutes. But the meetings drone on for an hour, only because they were scheduled to.

Your boss is well-intentioned, but he is so busy appeasing his own boss that your ideas are ignored. There's no clear guiding vision that you can fathom, other than to fix problems, put out fires, and figure out how to charge the customer more. Meanwhile, you watch your colleagues kiss your boss's ass to get ahead and try to look more valuable.

Information comes late and loud. In other words, problems are presented long after they should have been acknowledged and addressed, and these issues are always presented as "urgent." You frequently feel like you are the last person to learn about new initiatives.

You also feel like most of what you do is busy work. The e-mails keep piling up, and you keep hearing expressions such as "do more with less." You get meeting invitations you feel you can't decline, so you keep showing up at the meetings, and you keep working.

If you are among the majority of American workers, you work much more than forty hours per week—more hours than your counterparts in most other developed nations.[1] You are also working more hours in one of the wealthiest countries in the world that has no legal requirement to provide paid vacation. None. Canada, Japan, Germany, and the majority of Western European nations, by contrast, have a minimum of twenty (many have thirty or more) days of required paid vacation.[2]

The result is that you are stressed. And you feel guilty because you haven't taken time to exercise and deal with your stress. So you go for a run, and then feel guilty about taking time to exercise while the dishes pile up and the kids sit on the couch and watch Netflix.

Or does the following sound like you?

You work from home, coffee shops, or wherever you happen to be at the moment. You often feel at your most productive when you're *not* at the office. You go to the office when it matters to meet with colleagues, not to punch a clock. You are invited to conference calls and kept in the loop but attend only the ones relevant to your projects—the ones in which you are most interested and can make the biggest impact.

You take time to sleep and to exercise. Maybe you are the 5 a.m. boot-camp type, but you don't have to be; you can go for a run at 11 a.m. if you want to. You just take that time. You also take time to volunteer at your child's elementary school. You don't hide the fact that you contribute to your community when it fits into your schedule. The idea never occurred to you.

You have a great relationship with your boss. You don't dread interactions with her. Quite the opposite, you call her up any time you have an idea to share or need an opinion or support on a project. You always leave those interactions encouraged—even emboldened. She makes you feel like anything is possible. She generates energy in everyone around her.

Every time you sit in on a meeting with your boss, and your boss's boss, she is constantly giving away the credit and the limelight, while accepting accountability for anything that goes wrong.

The VP of sales asks, "We got a big customer win?" Your boss says, "Yes, but it wasn't me. It was our team that made it happen."

There's no gossip, and no trash-talking about the management over beers on Friday. And no fear of your job getting "bangalored" (outsourced). You live in a culture that is focused on outputs, not inputs—a work culture that is focused on results, not the volume of e-mails exchanged.

You have friends at work. You do things with one another's families for fun. You and your team create quality services and products, and you know it. You take pride in your work, and your colleagues do, too.

What's the difference between these two stories?

The difference is a series of small, incremental choices, made over time—starting with our own personal attitudes and daily behaviors. Those personal methods and mindsets then ripple out and affect the relationships we have with the people around us. We should live each day as we want to live the rest of our lives.

Let's start by exploring how practicing simple, intentional behaviors can lead to big impact—and how it's possible to change course even in the middle of a potential disaster.

Learning from Disaster

A few years ago I was the invited keynote speaker for a private conference in Toronto. It was one of my first big events. I knew the event director and was deeply grateful for the invitation. I prepared diligently. The ballroom was packed to the walls. I had published my first book and was just starting my work to share ideas onstage. I was knowledgeable, rehearsed, confident, and relaxed.

Onstage just before me was a professional comedian. She was

disarming and fun. She even sang. She was killing it. The crowd was totally enjoying her opening.

I was sitting near the stage next to the technician who was handling the audiovisual stuff. The comedian started to introduce me. She was warm, vibrant. She made a few jokes about my being American. Everyone laughed. She was just finishing my introduction when the tech guy next to me said, "Uh, hang on, your remote and the slides aren't working. Mmm, just go. Go and I'll fix it in a minute."

Good lord. The room was clapping for me. I gulped. My opening set piece was an in-depth story choreographed with a cascade of photographs and rich imagery. I designed the first few minutes to immerse the audience in a tale that would be a metaphor for my key points. But now I had no visuals.

I smiled. I walked the length of the stage to burn a few seconds, and said some ridiculous comment about the wonderful comedian. I had no idea what I just said. My head was clamoring. I could feel my field of vision start to close. I glanced at the technician, who clearly did not have his act together yet. Or maybe that was me.

I took a deep breath, smiled, found some friendly eyes in the audience, and launched into my story anyway. It was probably only a few seconds of dead air but it felt like an eternity. It worked. As I built the story, I warmed to it. I opened up, revisiting and punctuating each step of the journey. I started to own it. People leaned in. I had just jumped off a cliff and somehow found the rip cord.

In May 2013 I interviewed the magnificent speaker, writer, and marketing guru Seth Godin, who said that, if he ever gets that feeling of rising panic, he takes it as a reminder that he's in exactly the right place. He knows he is in a high-opportunity moment for learning and growth. What he means is that, when our palms get sweaty, our heart rate jumps, our hair stands on end, and we get nauseous, we are experiencing the symptoms of panic. They are also the conditions for challenging ourselves, seizing opportunity, and growing— if we choose to see it that way.

Simply focusing on our breathing can help get us through scary situations. It's true. The first thing we can do to lower our heart rate, calm our nerves, and open our mind again is breathe. Breathing is the body's built-in stress reliever. It's foundational to rebuilding calm. Simply breathing deeply can do everything from resetting our heart rate to changing the chemical composition of our blood. In the practice of yoga, focused breathing is called "pranayama," which literally means "control of the life force."

In my speaking example, I was able to recover from a potentially catastrophic and terrifying position and succeed. As we have explored in this book, getting from a place of anxiety, stress, and overwhelming confusion to a place of confidence and high performance takes small, incremental changes in behavior practiced over time. Reaching that place can start with something as simple as getting adequate rest.

Respecting Sleep

Captain Joseph Hazelwood was the centerpiece of the *Exxon Valdez* spill. He was allegedly drunk and incapable of operating the oil tanker competently at the time of the accident. But evidence later revealed Hazelwood wasn't even at the helm when the ship struck Bligh Reef in Prince William Sound. In fact, he was asleep in his bunk and had left the third mate, Gregory Cousins, at the helm. Cousins, along with most of the crew, was deeply sleep-deprived. Recent layoffs and overtime scheduling had left the crew exhausted.

Testimony before the National Transportation Safety Board revealed Cousins had been awake for "at least 18 hours" before the impact on Bligh Reef.[3]

Many experts believe Chernobyl to be the worst nuclear accident in history. Eighty-one miles north of Kiev in the Ukraine, the nuclear plant exploded on April 26, 1986, after workers spent the day attempting routine maintenance procedures to adhere to safety guidelines. Two explosions in quick succession blew the nuclear plant apart, killing two workers instantly. Over the following hours more died from acute radiation sickness.

While the official count is twenty-eight deaths due to the incident, experts believe thousands were affected. The site and surrounding area will likely be uninhabitable by humans for at least twenty thousand years. Reports show workers had been at their stations for thirteen hours or more before the explosion.[4]

Companies are recognizing the benefits of balance so much so that the latest sought-after company perk turns out to be the forty-hour workweek. Though it has been lost for the last few years in the always-on, digital-leash economy, the old-fashioned forty-hour workweek is returning in some companies. The latest change in company culture is a focus on limiting the number of hours people are expected to work. The Center for Creative Leadership recently did a study showing that professionals with smartphones (which today is like, everyone) are connected to their work up to eighteen hours a day, often checking their e-mail during the night.[5]

Ryan Sanders cofounded a staffing company, BambooHR, about five years ago. Tired (literally) of the go-go workaholic mentality he saw in the 1990s, he now *enforces* a forty-hour workweek at his company, which has specific policies to keep its employees from working overtime. If you are a BambooHR employee at your desk at 5:30 p.m., Sanders will probably visit you and ask what's up. But if your work problem persists, you could be fired. One of his software developers nearly lost her job after putting in a few sixty- to seventy-hour weeks.[6]

BambooHR understands what should be clear to all companies: when we are exhausted, our work quality deteriorates and our decision-making ability falls off a cliff. There's a reason that sleep deprivation is used as a form of torture. Psychological effects include hallucination, disorientation, recklessness, overoptimism, apathy, lethargy, and even social withdrawal. There is clear empirical data showing that healthcare professionals make a higher number of errors when sleep-deprived.[7]

The National Transportation Safety Board estimates up to one hundred thousand traffic accidents occur annually because of fatigue. We need to turn off our smartphones—shut them down—while we're driving. Nothing is so urgent that we should risk lives, including our own. And sleep will be a better performance booster than another night spent poring over spreadsheets until 11 p.m.

In July 2015, I interviewed Russ Cohn, CEO of Pantry Retail, a fast-growing company with the novel idea of providing high-quality, organic, perishable snacks in vending machines. The company manages its delicate inventory with radio-frequency identification (RFID) chips, which monitor and track sales of all items.[8] As an entrepreneur with a history of successful start-up companies, Cohn knows the stress of long days and urgent deadlines. And even he knows it doesn't make sense to push too hard. "All-nighters don't scale," he says. "Just because you've done two or ten all-nighters, it doesn't make it a sustainable strategy for growth."

Taking a Break from Technology

According to *Wikipedia,* "nomophobia" is the irrational fear (phobia) of "being without your mobile phone or being unable to use your phone for some reason."[9]

A recent study from the University of British Columbia by Kostadin Kushlev, a PhD candidate, with Elizabeth Dunn, concluded that, to reduce stress and increase overall productivity, the optimal number of times to check e-mail daily is three.[10] Ninety-two percent of Americans use e-mail, checking it up to fifteen times per day. Ironically, as Kushlev writes, "People find it difficult to resist the temptation of checking email, and yet resisting this temptation reduces their stress."

In the study, researchers asked 142 participants to limit their e-mail as much as possible for a week. During the following week, participants were invited to check their e-mail as often as they wanted. Eighteen people dropped out of the study almost as soon as it began, evidently unwilling to limit their e-mail intake.

During the course of the study, each day the 124 participants filled out a brief questionnaire about their stress levels, their sleep habits, and their subjective sense of well-being. They were asked questions such as the following:

- Today, how often have you felt nervous and stressed?
- Today, how often have you found that you could not cope with all the things that you had to do?
- Overall today, did you feel you got done the things at work that were most important to you?
- Overall today, how satisfied were you with what you accomplished at work?
- Overall, how would you rate the quality of your sleep last night?

During the phase in which they were asked to limit their e-mail activity as much as possible, participants reported significantly lower stress levels while engaged in activities that required sustained attention. In other words, when they had to persist at a particular activity with focus and energy, they were less distracted by the fact that they were not checking their e-mail.

The study concluded that our optimal sense of well-being, rest, and productivity comes from checking e-mail only three times per day—morning, midday, and late afternoon.

But of course it's not just e-mail; it's social media, texting, and other connective technologies that lead to a general sense of FOMO—fear of missing out. That fear of missing out becomes a consuming distraction in our lives, particularly when digital devices are nearby.

Putting Down Smartphones for Smarter Conversations

American adults are consuming more than eleven hours of digital media daily.[11] Keep in mind we are only awake sixteen to seventeen hours a day.

The consumption of digital media has been steadily increasing over the years for American kids, too. Today, on average, kids are spending more than seven hours immersed in "entertainment" screen time.[12] And that's outside of the screen time they may have at school, doing homework, or doing school-related activities on a computer.

It's true that sometimes it's nice to sit together at a coffee shop and absently chitchat about nothing important while we scroll through our devices. Together, yet apart. But more often, we all want our conversations to be meaningful, connected, deep, expressive, honest, intentional, substantial, and empathetic.

New research demonstrates that even the mere presence of a smartphone, in our hands or just sitting on the table between us, detracts from the quality of the conversation. That's right—even if we don't actively look at it, the simple presence of a smartphone detracts from the quality of the conversation. Simply the anticipation of a text or alert distracts us from meaningful interaction.

In that recent study, researchers Shalini Misra and her colleagues asked one hundred pairs of students to spend just ten minutes talking about either a casual, light topic or a deeper, more meaningful topic.[13] Meanwhile, an observing researcher nearby noted the amount of nonverbal behavior and the amount of eye contact. After the conversation took place, the observer asked questions related to the quality of the conversation itself. Participants were asked to qualify the "feelings of interpersonal connectedness" and "empathic concern" they experienced during the conversation. They were asked if they felt they could "really trust" their conversation partner and to what extent their conversation partner made an effort to understand the participant's thoughts and feelings.

The results were clear: "If either participant placed a mobile communication device on the table, or held it in their hand, during the course of the ten-minute conversation, the quality of the conversation was rated to be less fulfilling."

"Mobile phones hold symbolic meaning in advanced technological societies," the researchers concluded. "In their presence, people have the constant urge to seek out information, check for communication, and direct their thoughts to other people and worlds."

While the use of devices and technology that enable people to communicate digitally increases, face-to-face interaction decreases. According to Misra, "People who had conversations in the absence of mobile devices reported higher levels of empathetic concern."

Reclaiming Our Lives

How do we reclaim our lives from our devices? Meet William Powers.[14] Back in 2008, a digital lifetime ago, he, his wife, and his son were increasingly spending their evenings and weekends facing away from one another and spending hours deeply entranced by their screens, instead of talking to each other. Rather than simply interacting with one another, they were texting and e-mailing each other from across the house. They were also spending less and less time taking walks, enjoying the outdoors, and enjoying meaningful time with one another. As Powers describes in his book, "The goal is no longer to be 'in touch' but to erase the possibility of ever being out of touch."

The family decided to reclaim their lives from their devices. Ever since that decision almost ten years ago, they have been practicing something they call "selected disconnection." Each weekend they have an "Internet Sabbath." Starting late Friday evening and going through Sunday evening, they turn off the Wi-Fi, their smartphones, and their computers—they digitally disconnect.

They are certainly no Luddites. Powers is a researcher and journalist, and his wife is a novelist, so they both spend long hours at their computers, researching and writing. They are also both keenly aware that their ability to connect digitally gives them the freedom to work at home and make a living.

When they first started the experiment, Powers said, "It almost had an existential feeling of, 'I don't know who I am with the Internet gone.' But after a few months it hardened into a habit and we all began to realize we were gaining a lot from it."

Okay, so maybe the thought of totally disconnecting for two days is terrifying or unrealistic. But we can start with just an hour or two. Then, if we think it's a meaningful exercise for ourselves or our family, we can turn it into a whole evening. The worst-case scenario is we all learn something.

Taking Breaks When We're Busy

In 2014, when I was working at Skillsoft, a global online learning company, we did a survey in collaboration with Scott Eblin, leadership expert and author of *Overworked and Overwhelmed: The Mindfulness Alternative.*

In this short study, we asked busy professionals working in organizations larger than one thousand people how they spend their days—what time they wake up, how long their commute is, how many texts and e-mails they receive each day, how many meetings they sit through, how much exercise they get, and even how many cups of coffee they drink.

And then we asked a few questions about their sense of happiness, contentment, and productivity, and how much of the time they feel "at their best." The objective of the study was to understand how our daily behaviors affect our sense of well-being, productivity, and happiness—in our work, in our communities, and with our families.

Some of what we discovered may not surprise you, but one insight might: the busier we are in our work, the more we need to schedule, and take, regular breaks in our day in order to sustain high levels of happiness and productivity. The happiest and most productive professionals take regular mini-breaks throughout the day. And the more responsibility they have, the more important this practice becomes.

Digging into the survey data, we found that individual

contributors—that is, professionals who are not bosses, with no direct reports—suffer through the fewest meetings, received the lowest number of e-mails and texts (although 24 percent stated they receive more than fifty per day), had the shortest commute to work, and, for the most part, were good at leaving work at work. Only a third of this group spent more than forty hours a week in the office. These individual contributors also reported the fewest number of hours working outside of work—at home, in coffee shops, etc.

The majority of managers surveyed, in contrast, stated they had about two to six members on their team, received slightly higher volumes of e-mail and text messages regarding work than individual contributors, and, unsurprisingly, had to sit through a few more meetings each day. Managers also described slightly higher commuting distances, presumably because they were willing to travel farther for their position. This group is getting about the same amount of sleep as their individual-contributor counterparts, but dedicating a little more time each week to exercise.

Apparently gone are the days of executives having martini lunches and golfing twice a week, because in our survey the executive group overwhelmingly reported the highest volume of e-mails (31 percent say they receive more than a hundred), nearly twice as many meetings (many had up to six meetings per day!), and up to eighty hours of being connected to work each week, at the office and elsewhere. This group also travels the farthest to work, and, unsurprisingly, spends the greatest amount of time on airplanes. However, the executive group also reported the most hours dedicated to sleep and exercise.

Here's the piece of data that really surprised us: contributors and managers reported comparable levels of happiness and productivity, and comparable numbers of mini-breaks in their workday to refresh and recharge.

Meanwhile, we found that the greater the responsibility and obligations those surveyed have—in terms of meetings, direct reports, e-mail correspondence, travel, and other distractions—the more important the mental breaks become. In other words, those with the highest volume of distractions reported a much greater drop in productivity at work, and in satisfaction in all aspects of their lives, when they did *not* take mindful, intentional breaks during their day.

We should do our work, our family, and ourselves a favor: take a break. It's the first step toward finding the intentional time needed to begin more focused activities that will advance our goals of being more attuned to ourselves and those around us.

In this book, I'm suggesting that we can create more positive futures for ourselves, and for those around us, through small, incremental steps taken each day. You may think to yourself, "But I don't live in that world. I live in the world of rushing to meetings, and oceans of e-mails and stress!"

We can all move into a calmer, more fulfilling, and more impactful life. And the path to getting there is filled with small but highly intentional choices made consistently over time.

Here's the big idea in this book: we can't wait for seismic change to come from above. We can't wait for the phone to ring with the next big break, and we can't wait for someone else to elevate our "engagement." It's up to us. We lead by example. Along the way, we've explored how to take control of our lives and lead rather than waiting for our bosses—or for external circumstances—to direct us. It starts with each one of us and with the attitude and actions we take every day. You might think, "But my boss, but my deadlines..."

No, it starts with each one of us, and the attitude and action we take every day.

It is not intermittent, extraordinary actions that separate great leaders from everyone else; rather mindful leaders consistently do the simple things—like knowing when to take a break—extraordinarily well. When we start by doing the small things well, big things can happen.

Acknowledgments

I am deeply grateful to so many who have helped build this book.

Like other major projects in life, writing and publishing a book requires many people. Some I expect and rely on, and some appear unexpectedly, at just the right time, contributing small words of advice that help fill in parts of the puzzle, or anchor the whole process. Everyone is important, and for their efforts and perseverance, I am exceedingly grateful.

To begin, this would be a vastly different, and inferior, book without the conversations and interviews with those who greatly influenced my thinking: thank you, Rona Cant, for sharing your inspiring adventures; Paul Hiltz, for your remarkable servant leadership; Peter Senger, for your commitment and devotion to community; Amy Cuddy, for sharing your research and work to embolden our lives; Susan Cain, for inspiring our new company, which made this book possible; Scott Eblin, who leads his own life with honesty, humility, and authenticity; Howard Behar, who shared stories from his adventures at Starbucks; Teresa Amabile, for helping us all make small steps of progress in our lives; Gene and Jill Klein, for sharing your astonishing true tale of Holocaust survival; and Hap Klopp, for your generosity of ideas and expansive wisdom.

Thank you also to Scott Turicchi, Tom DiDonato, Bashar Nejdawi, Sue Mahony, Victor Cho, Mary Waller, Seth Godin, and

Liz Wiseman. You likely don't know each other, yet you all contributed thoughts from your own work, in vastly different worlds, that complement and reinforce the ideas in this book.

Thank you to my editor, Pam Owen, who skillfully brought this manuscript into coherence. Thank you, Erika Heilman, Jill Friedlander, and all of the wonderful, hardworking, caring, and conscientious people at Bibliomotion. Thank you, Lisa DiMona, my literary agent, who has an uncanny knack for knowing what to do when I don't. Thank you, Lori Ames and the good people at PRFreelancer, who are giving this book the reach and buoyancy to help people around the world find it, often in places I would have never thought to put it.

Thank you, Amy, my wonderful wife, and Charlie, Will, and Annie, our inspiring children. Without your constant love and distraction, this book would have been finished in half the time, but would have been half as good.

Notes

Introduction

1. "John Wooden: First, How to Put on Your Socks," *Newsweek* online, October 24, 1999, http://www.newsweek.com/john-wooden-first-how -put-your-socks-167942.
2. "John Wooden Interview," Academy of Achievement, February 27, 1999, http://www.achievement.org/autodoc/page/woo0int-4.

Chapter 1

1. Albert Bandura, "Self-efficacy," in *Encyclopedia of Human Behavior,* vol. 4, ed. V. S. Ramachaudran, (New York: Academic Press), 71–81. Reprinted in *Encyclopedia of Mental Health,* ed. H. Friedman (San Diego: Academic Press, 1998).
2. "The Impostor Syndrome," Caltech Counseling Center, accessed January 19, 2016, https://counseling.caltech.edu/general/Infoand Resources/Impostor.
3. Olivia Fox Cabane, *The Charisma Myth: How Anyone Can Master the Art and Science of Personal Magnetism* (New York: Portfolio, 2013), also available at https://books.google.com/books?id=WBVVgK0tYO kC&pg=PT29&lpg=PT29&dq=How+many+of+you+in+here+feel +that+you+are+the+one+mistake+that+the+admissions+committee +made&source=bl&ots=qit7HsujEF&sig=JUg72FHfeTWGT759K r4AHBLctz0&hl=en&sa=X&ved=0ahUKEwia_rig29bKAhVN7m MKHcrADmoQ6AEIHTAA#v=onepage&q=How%20many%20 of%20you%20in%20here%20feel%20that%20you%20are%20

the%20one%20mistake%20that%20the%20admissions%20
committee%20made&f=false.

4. Susan Pinker, *The Sexual Paradox: Men, Women and the Real Gender Gap* (New York: Scribner, 2009), 184.

5. Valerie Young, *The Secret Thoughts of Successful Women: Why Capable People Suffer from the Impostor Syndrome and How to Thrive in Spite of It* (New York: Crown Business, 2011), 38.

6. Marie Reine Haddad, "Impostor Syndrome: No You Are Not a Fraud," NICHD Collection, Eunice Kennedy Shriver National Institute of Child Health and Human Development, April 2, 2014, https://science.nichd.nih.gov/confluence/display/newsletter/2014/04/02/Impostor+Syndrome%3A+No+You+Are+Not+a+Fraud.

7. Amy Cuddy, "Your Body Language Shapes Who You Are," TED Talk, June 2012, http://www.ted.com/talks/amy_cuddy_your_body_language_shapes_who_you_are.

8. Laurence Gonzales, *Deep Survival: Who Lives, Who Dies, and Why* (New York: W. W. Norton & Company, 2003), also available at https://books.google.com/books?id=KQaySo3l6j0C&dq=M.+Ephimia+Morphew+scuba&source=gbs_navlinks_s.

9. Gonzales, *Deep Survival*, 287.

10. Al Siebert, Kristin Pintarich, and Molly Siebert, *The Survivor Personality: Why Some People Are Stronger, Smarter, and More Skillful at Handling Life's Difficulties—And How You Can Be, Too* (New York: Perigee, 2010), also available at https://books.google.com/books?id=8n5YAuG2xB4C&pg=PT136&dq=The+best+survivors+spend+almost+no+time,+especially+in+emergencies,+getting+upset+about+what+has+been+lost,+or+feeling+distressed+about+things&hl=en&sa=X&ved=0ahUKEwih_puEqMDJAhXMQCYKHQU6CKwQ6AEIIzAB#v=onepage&q=The%20best%20survivors%20spend%20almost%20no%20time%2C%20especially%20in%20emergencies%2C%20getting%20upset%20about%20what%20has%20been%20lost%2C%20or%20feeling%20distressed%20about%20things&f=false.

11. Kelly McGonigal, "How to Make Stress Your Friend," TEDGlobal 2013, TED Talk, June 2013, http://www.ted.com/talks/kelly_mcgonigal_how_to_make_stress_your_friend?language=en&utm_source=Shawn%27

s+Blog+Updates&utm_campaign=0657f5a034-RSS_campaign&utm_medium=email&utm_term=0_76214e7fb1-0657f5a034-33416069.
12. Ben Thompson, "Joe S. Simpson," *Bad Ass of the Week*, accessed November 29, 2015, http://www.badassoftheweek.com/simpson.html.
13. Joe Simpson, *Touching the Void: The True Story of One Man's Survival* (New York: HarperCollins Publishers, 1988).
14. GCC Insights, "Stress—The Hidden Threat in Every Workplace," *GCC Blog*, posted March 5, 2015, https://www.gettheworldmoving.com/blog/stress-insights-report.
15. "Dangerously Stressful Work Environments Force Workers to Seek New Employment," Monster, accessed December 1, 2015, http://www.monster.com/about/a/Dangerously-Stressful-Work-Environments-Force-Workers-to-Seek-New-Empl4162014-D3126696.
16. Jodi Kantor and David Streitfeld, "Inside Amazon: Wrestling Big Ideas in a Bruising Workplace," *New York Times*, August 16, 2015, http://www.nytimes.com/2015/08/16/technology/inside-amazon-wrestling-big-ideas-in-a-bruising-workplace.html.
17. Richard Wiseman, *The Luck Factor* (Santa Monica, CA: Miramax, 2003).
18. Bronnie Ware, *The Top Five Regrets of the Dying: A Life Transformed by the Dearly Departing* (Carlsbad, CA: Hay House, 2012).

Chapter 2

1. David Winner, "ESPN FC: Beautiful Game. Beautiful Mind," ESPN, May 16, 2012, http://espn.go.com/IndexPages/news/story?id=7938409.
2. Christopher Clarey, "Olympians Use Imagery as Mental Training," *New York Times*, February 22, 2014, http://www.nytimes.com/2014/02/23/sports/olympics/olympians-use-imagery-as-mental-training.html?_r=0.
3. Ibrahim Senay, Dolores Albarracín, and Kenji Noguchi, "Motivating Goal-Directed Behavior Through Introspective Self-Talk: The Role of the Interrogative Form of Simple Future Tense," *Psychological Science* 21 (2010), 499–504, doi:10.1177/0956797610364751.
4. Mark Muraven, "Building Self-Control Strength: Practicing Self-Control Leads to Improved Self-Control Performance," *Journal of*

Experimental Social Psychology 46 (2010): 465–468, doi:10.1016/
j.jesp.2009.12.011.

5. NFL, "Odell Beckham Makes Catch of the Year!" YouTube video, 1:15, posted January 25, 2015, https://www.youtube.com/watch?v=zxbz3DDQzHU.

6. Dan Coyle, "The Power of High-Leverage Practice," *The Talent Code* blog, accessed November 24, 2015, http://thetalentcode.com/2014/11/24/the-power-of-high-leverage-practice.

7. Dana R. Carney, Amy J. C. Cuddy, and Andy J. Yap, "Power Posing: Brief Nonverbal Displays Affect Neuroendocrine Levels and Risk Tolerance," *Psychological Science* 21 (2010): 1363–1368, doi:10.1177/0956797610383437.

8. Rebecca Shannonhouse, "Is Your Boss Making You Sick?" *Washington Post*, October 20, 2014, https://www.washingtonpost.com/national/health-science/is-your-boss-making-you-sick/2014/10/20/60cd5d44-2953-11e4-8593-da634b334390_story.html.

9. Anna Nyberg et al., "Managerial Leadership and Ischaemic Heart Disease Among Employees: The Swedish WOLF Study," *Occupational and Environmental Medicine* 66 (2009), 51–55, doi:10.1136/oem.2008.039362.

10. Jeffrey Liker, *The Toyota Way: 14 Management Principles from the World's Greatest Manufacturer* (New York: McGraw Hill Professional, 2003).

11. Ethan S. Bernstein, "The Transparency Paradox: A Role for Privacy in Organizational Learning and Operational Control," *Administrative Science Quarterly* 57 (2012): 181–216, doi:10.1177/0001839212453028.

12. Will Durant, *The Story of Philosophy: The Lives and Opinions of the World's Greatest Philosophers* (New York: Simon & Schuster/Pocket Books, 1991, originally published 1926).

13. Laura Hale, "Generation Grit: Retro-Inspired Action Figures," Kickstarter, accessed December 3, 2015, https://www.kickstarter.com/projects/1882390019/generation-grit.

14. "Time to Practice What We Preach," *Generation Grit* blog, July 3, 2014, http://www.generationgrit.com/blog3/2014/7/2/time-to-practice-what-we-preach.

15. Laura M. Padilla-Walker, Randal D. Day, William Justin Dyer, and Brent C. Black, "'Keep on Keeping On, Even When It's Hard!': Predictors and Outcomes of Adolescent Persistence," *The Journal of Early Adolescence* 33 (2013): 433–457 (first published on June 18, 2012), doi:10.1177/0272431612449387.

16. Mikaela Conley, "Persistence Is Learned from Fathers, Says Study," ABC News, June 15, 2012, http://abcnews.go.com/Health/persistence -learned-fathers-study/story?id=16571927.

17. Dina Gachman, "Stephen King: His Ten Best Quotes on Writing," SSN, October 16, 2013, http://www.ssninsider.com/stephen-king -his-ten-best-quotes-on-writing.

Chapter 3

1. Albert Bandura and Nancy E. Adams, "Analysis of Self-Efficacy Theory of Behavioral Change," *Cognitive Therapy and Research* 1 (1977): 287–310, doi:10.1016/0146-6402(78)90002-4.

2. Claudia M. Mueller and Carol S. Dweck, "Praise for Intelligence Can Undermine Children's Motivation and Performance," *Journal of Personality and Social Psychology* 75 (1998): 33–52, doi:http://dx.doi .org/10.1037/0022-3514.75.1.33.

3. Jason S. Moser, Hans S. Schroder, Carrie Heeter, Tim P. Moran, and Yu-Hao Lee, "Mind Your Errors: Evidence for a Neural Mechanism Linking Growth Mind-Set to Adaptive Posterror Adjustments," *Psychological Science* 22 (2011): 1484; originally published online October 31, 2011, doi:10.1177/0956797611419520.

4. Carol Dweck in an interview by Taavo Godtfredsen, Skillsoft Corporation, April 2014, Stanford University.

5. Grayson Schaffer, "The Toughest Woman on Two Wheels," *Outside* online, April 29, 2015, http://www.outsideonline.com/1970876/ toughest-woman-two-wheels.

6. Kevin Lynch, "Record Holder Profile: Juliana Buhring—Fastest Circumnavigation by Bicycle," Guinness World Records, November 6, 2013, http://www.guinnessworldrecords.com/news/2013/ 11/record-holder-profile-juliana-buhring-%E2%80%93-fastest-circu mnavigation-by-bicycle-52724.

7. Grayson Schaffer, "The Toughest Woman on Two Wheels."
8. Marguerite Del Giudice, "Grit Trumps Talent and IQ: A Story Every Parent (and Educator) Should Read," *National Geographic*, October 14, 2014, http://news.nationalgeographic.com/news/2014/10/141015-angela-duckworth-success-grit-psychology-self-control-science-nginnovators.
9. A. L. Duckworth, C. Peterson, M. D. Matthews, and D. R. Kelly, "Grit: Perseverance and Passion for Long-term Goals, *Journal of Personality and Social Psychology* 9 (2007): 1087-1101. Download the "Grit Scale" from https://docs.google.com/viewer?url=https://www.sas.upenn.edu/~duckwort/images/12-item%20Grit%20Scale.05312011.pdf.
10. Lauren Eskreis et al., "The Grit Effect: Predicting Retention in the Military, the Workplace, School and Marriage," *Frontiers in Psychology*, February 3, 2014, doi:10.3389/fpsyg.2014.00036.
11. Monika Hamori, Jie Cao, and Burak Koyuncu, "Why Top Young Managers Are in a Nonstop Job Hunt," *Harvard Business Review*, July–August 2012, https://hbr.org/2012/07/why-top-young-managers-are-in-a-nonstop-job-hunt/ar/1.
12. Nicole Fallon, "Solving the Mystery of Gen Y Job Hoppers," *Business News Daily*, August 22, 2014, businessnewsdaily.com/7012-millennial-job-hopping.html.
13. "Study Highlights: Work-Life Is Harder Worldwide," EY (Ernst & Young Global Limited), accessed December 2, 2015, http://www.ey.com/US/en/About-us/Our-people-and-culture/EY-study-highlights-work-life-is-harder-worldwide#.Vl8BidKrR0u. Based on a survey conducted between November 20, 2014, and January 14, 2015.

Chapter 4

1. Teresa Amabile and Steven Kramer, *The Progress Principle: Using Small Wins to Ignite Joy, Engagement, and Creativity at Work* (Cambridge, MA: Harvard Business Review Press, 2011).
2. Adam Grant, "Finding the Hidden Value in Your Network," Blog, *HuffPost Business*, updated August 18, 2013, http://www.huffingtonpost.com\adam-grant\finding-the-hidden-value-_1_b_3458536.html.

3. Harold Nicolson, *Dwight Morrow* (New York: Harcourt, Brace and Company, 1935), 52.

4. Brooks Barnes, "The Voice Behind Mick (and Others)," *New York Times*, June 7, 2013, http://www.nytimes.com/2013/06/09/movies/the-voice-behind-mick-and-others.html.

5. Lyndsey Parker, "Judith Hill on Jamming with Prince, Remembering Michael Jackson, and What 'The Voice' Taught Her About America," Yahoo Music, October 21, 2015, https://www.yahoo.com/music/s/judith-hill-on-jamming-with-prince-remembering-004526004.html.

6. Felix Warneken and Michael Tomasello, "The Roots of Human Altruism," *British Journal of Psychology* 100 (2009): 455–471, doi:10.1348/000712608X379061.

7. Lorenzo Coviello et al., "Detecting Emotional Contagion in Massive Social Networks," *PLOS ONE*, March 12, 2014, doi:10.1371/journal.pone.0090315.

8. David M. Buss, "Human Mate Selection," *American Scientist* 73 (1985): 47–51, https://www.researchgate.net/profile/David_Buss/publication/233820651_Human_mate_selection/links/00b7d52fe2ac5a9eed000000.pdf.

9. Ibid.

10. Philip Brickman, Dan Coates, and Ronnie Janoff-Bulman, "Lottery Winners and Accident Victims: Is Happiness Relative?" *Journal of Personality and Social Psychology* 36 (1978): 917–927; doi:10.1037/00223514.36.8.917.

11. Robert Emmons, "How Gratitude Can Help You Through Hard Times," Greater Good, May 13, 2013, http://greatergood.berkeley.edu/article/item/how_gratitude_can_help_you_through_hard_times.

12. Jeffrey J. Froh and Giacomo Bono, "Gratitude in Adolescence: An Understudied Virtue," available at https://docs.google.com/viewer?url=http://people.hofstra.edu/jeffrey_j_froh/spring%202010%20web/Gratitude%20in%20Adolescence%20Encyclopedia%20Entry_sent%20to%20Roger_R1_12.29.09.pdf.

13. Po Bronson and Ashley Merryman, *NurtureShock: New Thinking About Children* (New York: Grand Central Publishing, 2009), also available at https://books.google.com/books?id=AlknZbhbUPAC&pg=PT93&lpg

=PT93&dq=study+writing+letters+of+gratitude+froh&source=bl&o
ts=2m7RCNOeEy&sig=7DzO8i1dZvZkA0RnSqlav0fR4KA&hl=en
&sa=X&ei=G-p8UteFKsfC4AOXzID4Cg#v=onepage&q=study%20
writing%20letters%20of%20gratitude%20froh&f=false.

14. Norman Cousins, *Anatomy of an Illness: As Perceived by the Patient*
    (New York: W. W. Norton & Company, 1979).

15. Cousins, *Anatomy of an Illness*, 29.

16. "AIG—Laughing Baby Ethan," Tvspots.tv, posted March 3, 2011,
    http://www.tvspots.tv/video/52586/aig--laughing-baby-ethan.

17. Erik Weihenmayer, *The Adversity Advantage: Turning Everyday Strug-
    gles into Everyday Greatness* (New York: Touchstone, 2007).

Chapter 5

1. Daniel Kahneman, *Thinking Fast and Slow* (New York: Farrar, Straus
   and Giroux, 2011), 212.

2. Daniel Gilbert, *Stumbling on Happiness* (New York: Vintage, 2007).

3. Merck KGaA Darmstadt, "State of Curiosity: Executive Overview," September 9, 2015, http://www.125yearssmartertogether.com/wp-content/
   uploads/2015/09/1509_Merck_Executive-Summary_R8a1.pdf.

4. Adobe, "State of Create: Global Benchmark Study on Attitudes and
   Beliefs About Creativity at Work, School and Home," April 2012,
   http://www.adobe.com/aboutadobe/pressroom/pdfs/Adobe_State
   _of_Create_Global_Benchmark_Study.pdf.

5. Dale Carnegie Training, *The 5 Essential People Skills: How to Assert
   Yourself, Listen to Others, and Resolve Conflicts* (New York: Touchstone, 2009), 87–88.

6. "Study Reveals That Many People Are Oblivious to How They
   Come Across to Counterparts, Colleagues," June 30, 2014, Phys.org,
   http://phys.org/news/2014-06-reveals-people-oblivious-counterparts
   -colleagues.html.

7. "Bob Sutton: Power Poisoning," YouTube video, 1:51, posted by
   "Stanford eCorner," November 23, 2010, https://www.youtube.com/
   watch?v=TDBWg9e_cZk.

8. Robert C. Litchfield, Cameron M. Ford, and Richard J. Gentry, "Linking Individual Creativity to Organizational Innovation,"

The Journal of Creative Behavior 49 (2015): 279–294, doi:10.1002/jocb.65.

9. Paul Piff, "Does Money Make You Mean?" TED Talk, October 2013, https://www.ted.com/talks/paul_piff_does_money_make_you_mean?language=en.

10. Phyllis Guest, "The Growing Problem of Workplace Bullying," November 17, 2011, Workplace Bullying Institute, http://www.work placebullying.org/guest.

Chapter 6

1. K. Anders Ericsson and Neil Charness, "Expert Performance: Its Structure and Acquisition," *American Psychologist*, 49 (1994): 725–747, http://dx.doi.org/10.1037/0003-066X.49.8.725.

2. Brooke N. Macnamara, David Z. Hambrick, Frederick L. Oswald, "Deliberate Practice and Performance in Music, Games, Sports, Education, and Professions: A Meta-Analysis," *Psychological Science*, 25 (2014): 1608–1618, doi:10.1177/0956797614535810.

3. At the Hyatt Hotel, New York City.

4. Michigan State University, "Abusive Leadership Infects Entire Team," ScienceDaily, August 20, 2014, http://www.sciencedaily.com/releases /2014/08/140820091703.htm.

5. Robert Sutton, "Is Your Future Boss a Demeaning Creep?" Bloomberg Business, June 23, 2015, http://www.businessweek.com/business_at _work/bad_bosses/archives/2008/06/is_your_future.html.

6. Lynn Taylor, "Bad Boss Behaviors Rise Up to 50%; Says Five-Year Comparative Study," PR Newswire, October 7, 2009, http://www .prnewswire.com/news-releases/bad-boss-behaviors-rise-up-to-50 -says-five-year-comparative-study-63685702.html.

7. "50 Common Signs and Symptoms of Stress," The American Institute of Stress, http://www.stress.org/stress-effects.

Chapter 7

1. Hakan Ozcelik and Sigal Barsade, "Work Loneliness and Employee Performance," *Academy of Management Proceedings*, January 2011 (Meeting Abstract Supplement): 1–6, doi:10.5465/AMBPP.2011.65869714.

2. Kenji Yoshino and Christie Smith, "Uncovering Talent: A New Model for Inclusion," Deloitte University Leadership Center for Inclusion, updated December 6, 2013, https://www2.deloitte.com/content/dam/Deloitte/us/Documents/about-deloitte/us-inclusion-uncovering-talent-paper.pdf.

3. Louise C. Hawkley et al., "Loneliness Predicts Increased Blood Pressure: Five-Year Cross-Lagged Analyses in Middle-Aged and Older Adults," *Psychology and Aging*, 25 (2010): 132–141, doi:10.1037/a0017805.

4. Athletic shoes originally associated with the Chuck Taylor All-Stars sneaker, the most successful-selling basketball shoe in history, according to *Wikipedia*, accessed February 4, 2016, https://en.wikipedia.org/wiki/Chuck_Taylor_(salesman).

5. http://www2.deloitte.com/content/dam/Deloitte/us/Documents/about-deloitte/us-inclusion-uncovering-talent-paper.pdf.

6. Roy F. Baumeister et al., "Bad Is Stronger Than Good," *Review of General Psychology*, 5 (2001): 323–370, doi:10.1037//1089-2680.5.4.323.

7. Anna-Kaisa Newheisera and Manuela Barretoa, "Hidden Costs of Hiding Stigma: Ironic Interpersonal Consequences of Concealing a Stigmatized Identity in Social Interactions," *Journal of Experimental Social Psychology*, 52 (2014): 58–70, doi:10.1016/j.jesp.2014.01.002.

8. Matt Ridley, "When Ideas Have Sex," TED Talk, July 2010, http://www.ted.com/talks/matt_ridley_when_ideas_have_sex.

9. Kendra Cherry, "The Asch Conformity Experiments," About Health, updated May 17, 2015, http://psychology.about.com/od/classicpsychologystudies/p/conformity.htm.

10. Charles Efferson, Rafael Lalive, Peter J. Richerson, Richard McElreath, Mark Lubell, "Conformists and Mavericks: The Empirics of Frequency-Dependent Cultural Transmission," *Evolution and Human Behavior* 29 (2008): 56–64, doi:http://dx.doi.org/10.1016/j.evolhumbehav.2007.08.003.

11. Bruce Keppel, "Pacific Bell Calls Halt to Disputed Training Plan," October 30, 1987, *Los Angeles Times*, http://articles.latimes.com/1987-10-30/business/fi-11672_1_pacific-bell.

12. Patricia T. O'Conner and Stewart Kellerman, "Out of Pocket, Revisited," *Grammarphobia Blog*, April 16, 2010, http://www.grammar phobia.com/blog/2010/04/out-of-pocket-revisited.html.

Chapter 8

1. Merriam-Webster, http://www.merriam-webster.com/dictionary/mind fulness.

2. Richard Chambers and Margie Ulbrick, *Mindful Relationships: Creating Genuine Connection with Ourselves and Others* (Wollombi, NSW, Australia: Exisle, forthcoming), also available at https://books.google .com/books?id=IqZdCwAAQBAJ&pg=PP1&dq=ulbrick+mindfu l+relationships&hl=en&sa=X&ved=0ahUKEwj65p-65dzKAhUB -WMKHWtzBAIQ6AEIHTAA#v=onepage&q=ulbrick%20mind ful%20relationships&f=false.

3. "Take Notes by Hand for Better Long-Term Comprehension," Association for Psychological Science, accessed February 4, 2016, http://www.psychologicalscience.org/index.php/news/releases/take -notes-by-hand-for-better-long-term-comprehension.html.

4. Scott Eblin, *Overworked and Overwhelmed: The Mindfulness Alternative* (Hoboken, NJ: Wiley, 2014).

5. "Mindfulness in the Age of Complexity," *Harvard Business Review*, March 2014, https://hbr.org/2014/03/mindfulness-in-the-age-of-complexity.

6. Hap Klopp, *Conquering the North Face: An Adventure in Leadership* (Bloomington, IN: iUniverse, 2012), 93.

7. Michal Austin, "Texting While Driving: How Dangerous Is It?" *Car and Driver*, June 2009, http://www.caranddriver.com/features/ texting-while-driving-how-dangerous-is-it.

8. Eyal Ophira, Clifford Nass, and Anthony D. Wagner, "Cognitive Control in Media Multitaskers," *Proceedings of the National Academy of Sciences* 106 (2009): 15583–15587, doi:10.1073/pnas.0903620106.

9. Christopher Reeve, *Nothing Is Impossible: Reflections on a New Life* (New York: Ballantine Books, 2004), 15.

10. "The Heroics of Captain Sully and the 'Miracle on the Hudson,'" Patrick Smith's Ask the Pilot, accessed January 30, 2016, http://www .askthepilot.com/questionanswers/sully-and-heroics.

11. "Staff Ride to the South Canyon Fire," Wildland Fire Leadership Development Program, accessed December 2, 2015, http://www.fire leadership.gov/toolbox/staffride/library_staff_ride9.html.

12. "Mann Gulch Fire, 1949," The Forest History Society, accessed December 2, 2015, http://www.foresthistory.org/ASPNET/Policy/ Fire/FamousFires/MannGulch.aspx.

13. "1910 Fires: Edward Pulaski," U.S. Forest Service website, accessed December 2, 2015, http://www.fs.usda.gov/detail/r1/learning/history -culture/?cid=stelprdb5122876.

14. Jenny W. Rudolph and J. Bradley Morrison, "Confidence, Error, and Inge- nuity in Diagnostic Problem Solving: Clarifying the Role of Exploration and Exploitation," Draft Version 1, Winter 2007, http://people.brandeis .edu/~bmorriso/documents/ConfidenceErrorIngenuityinDx.pdf.

Chapter 9

1. Val Kinjerski and Berna J. Skrypnek, "Creating Organizational Conditions That Foster Employee Spirit at Work," *Leadership & Organization Devel- opment Journal* 27 (2006): 280–295, doi:10.1108/01437730610666037.

2. "Meghan Vogel, Ohio Track Star, Carries Runner Across Finish Line at State Competition," YouTube video, 0:45, posted by "New Everyday News!" August 24, 2012, https://www.youtube.com/watch?v=H1F9hRFUr6I.

3. Martin E. P. Seligman, *Authentic Happiness: Using the New Positive Psychology to Realize Your Potential for Lasting Fulfillment* (New York: Free Press, 2002), 167.

4. "The Three Dimensions of a Complete Life," Martin Luther King Jr. and the Global Freedom Struggle, last accessed February 1, 2016, http:// kingencyclopedia.stanford.edu/encyclopedia/documentsentry/ doc_the_three_dimensions_of_a_complete_life.

5. Peter Ferdinand Drucker, *The Effective Executive* (New York: Harper & Row, 1967), 57.

6. J. Richard Hackman, "Leading Teams: Setting the Stage for Great Performances—The Five Keys to Successful Teams," Harvard Business School Working Knowledge, July 15, 2002, http://hbswk. hbs.edu/archive/2996.html.

7. Nicole Frost et al., "From Our Readers: How Mentorship Affects Retention Rates of New Nurses," *American Nurse Today* 8 (2013), http://www.americannursetoday.com/from-our-readers-how -mentorship-affects-retention-rates-of-new-nurses.

8. Jonah E. Rockoff, *Does Mentoring Reduce Turnover and Improve Skills of New Employees? Evidence from Teachers in New York City,* Working Paper 13868, NBER Working Paper Series, National Bureau of Economic Research, March 2008, 33, doi:10.3386/w13868.

9. James W. Pennebaker, *Opening Up: The Healing Power of Expressing Emotions* (New York: The Guilford Press, 1997), 3.

10. Rob Cross, Jane C. Linder, Andrew Parker, "Charged Up: Managing the Energy That Drives Innovation," presented at the Network Roundtable at the University of Virginia, http://www.robcross.org/ pdf/roundtable/energy_and_innovation.pdf.

11. Charles Derber, *The Pursuit of Attention: Power and Ego in Everyday Life* (Oxford: Oxford University Press, 2000).

12. Gretchen Spreitzer and Christine Porath, "Creating Sustainable Performance," *Harvard Business Review*, January–February 2012, https:// hbr.org/2012/01/creating-sustainable-performance.

Chapter 10

1. Luke Swartz, *Overwhelmed by Technology: How Did User Interface Failures on Board the USS* Vincennes *Lead to 290 Dead?*, 2001, http:// xenon.stanford.edu/~lswartz/vincennes.pdf.

2. "How It Works," Holacracy, accessed January 29, 2016, http://www .holacracy.org/how-it-works.

3. Fred R. H. Zijlstra, Mary J. Waller, and Sybil I. Phillips, "Setting the Tone: Early Interaction Patterns in Swift Starting Teams As a Predictor of Effectiveness," *European Journal of Work and Organizational Psychology* 21 (2012), doi:10.1080/1359432X.2012.690399.

4. Bruce S. Feiler, *The Secrets of Happy Families: Improve Your Mornings, Rethink Family Dinner, Fight Smarter, Go Out and Play, and Much More*, Kindle edition (New York, NY: William Morrow, 2013).

5. Paolo Guenzi and Dino Ruta, *Leading Teams: Tools and Techniques for Successful Team Leadership from the Sports World* (Hoboken, NJ: Jossey-Bass, 2013).

6. Rona Cant, *Snow, Sleds and Silence: The Story of the Nordkapp Expedition* (Faringdon, Oxfordshire: Libri Publishing, 2012).

7. Rebecca Shannonhouse, "Is Your Boss Making You Sick?," *Washington Post*, October 20, 2014, available at https://www.washingtonpost.com/ national/health-science/is-your-boss-making-you-sick/2014/10/20/ 60cd5d44-2953-11e4-8593-da634b334390_story.html.

Chapter 11

1. "Understanding the Impact of Positive Deviance in Work Organizations," University of Michigan's Ross School of Business, July 4, 2004, https://michiganross.umich.edu/rtia-articles/understanding-impact -positive-deviance-work-organizations.

2. Steve Gruenert and Todd Whitaker, *School Culture Rewired: How to Define, Assess, and Transform It* (Alexandria, VA: ASCD, 2015).

3. Russell Hotten, "Volkswagen: The Scandal Explained," BBC News, December 11, 2015, http://www.bbc.com/news/business-34324772.

4. Diane Vaughan, *The Challenger Launch Decision: Risky Technology, Culture, and Deviance at NASA* (Chicago: University of Chicago Press, 1997).

5. Vaughan, *The Challenger Launch Decision*, 156, also available at https://books.google.com/books?id=erYjCwAAQBAJ&q=o-rings#v =onepage&q=Orings&f=false.

6. Howard Berkes, "30 Years After Explosion, Challenger Engineer Still Blames Himself," NPR, updated January 29, 2016, http://www.npr .org/sections/thetwo-way/2016/01/28/464744781/30-years-after -disaster-challenger-engineer-still-blames-himself.

7. Howard Berkes, "Remembering Roger Boisjoly: He Tried to Stop Shuttle Challenger Launch," updated February 7, 2012, http://www .npr.org/sections/thetwo-way/2012/02/06/146490064/remembering -roger-boisjoly-he-tried-to-stop-shuttle-challenger-launch.

8. Dario Maestripieri, "What Monkeys Can Teach Us About Human Behavior: From Facts to Fiction," *Psychology Today*, posted March

20, 2012, https://www.psychologytoday.com/blog/games-primates
-play/201203/what-monkeys-can-teach-us-about-human-behavior
-facts-fiction.

9. Richard Pascale, Jerry Sternin, and Monique Sternin, *The Power of Positive Deviance: How Unlikely Innovators Solve the World's Toughest Problems* (Cambridge, MA: Harvard Business Review Press, 2010).

10. "Elm," Arbor Day Foundation, accessed January 29, 2016, https://www.arborday.org/programs/nationaltree/elm.cfm.

11. "Dutch Elm Disease," *Wikipedia,* accessed January 15, 2016, https://en.wikipedia.org/wiki/Dutch_elm_disease.

12. Cahal Milmo, "Has a Cure Been Found for Dutch Elm Disease?," *The Independent,* June 7, 2010, http://www.independent.co.uk/environment/nature/has-a-cure-been-found-for-dutch-elm-disease-1994102.html.

13. "Healthcare-associated Infections (HAI) Progress Report," Centers for Disease Control and Prevention, last updated March 3, 2015, http://www.cdc.gov/hai/progress-report.

14. Arvind Singhal and Karen Greiner (abridged version prepared by Prucia Buscell), "Do What You Can, with What You Have, Where You Are: A Quest to Eliminate MRSA at the VA Pittsburgh Healthcare System," Plexus Institute, *Deeper Learning* 1 (2007), 5, http://c.ymcdn.com/sites/www.plexusinstitute.org/resource/collection/6528ed29-9907-4bc7-8d00-8dc907679fed/VAPHS_PD_MRSA_Story_Condensed_-_Final.pdf.

15. "Healthcare-associated Infections (HAI) Progress Report," Centers for Disease Control and Prevention, last updated March 3, 2015, http://www.cdc.gov/hai/progress-report.

16. James Pat Smith, "Leadership and Mission in Resilient Organizations: Hancock Bank As a Case Study," Community and Regional Resilience Institute, last viewed January 12, 2016, http://www.resilientus.org/wp-content/uploads/2013/03/GP_Resilience_Essay_Hancock_Bank_Final_8409_1249429792.pdf.

17. Fred Hassan, *Reinvent: A Leader's Playbook for Serial Success* (New York: Jossey-Bass, 2013), also available at https://books.google.com/books?id=6ywwofiaw18C&pg=PT130&lpg=PT130&dq=fred+hassan+If+you+are+in+a+position+of+making+a+sale+and+doing+something

+you+are+not+comfortable+with%E2%80%94something+you+wo
n%27t+feel+proud+of+later&source=bl&ots=U_nNCx0Hp2&sig
=OnVFceU8E3Gm4sHSd-F37zg4mcE&hl=en&sa=X&ved=0ahUK
Ewi39v7t0JDKAhVH8j4KHSO0C5YQ6AEIHTAA#v=onepage&q
=if%20you%20are%20in%20a%20position&f=false.

Chapter 12

1. Joan C. Williams and Heather Boushey, "The Three Faces of Work-Family Conflict: The Poor, the Professionals, and the Missing Middle," Center for American Progress, January 25, 2010, https://www.americanprogress.org/issues/labor/report/2010/01/25/7194/the-three-faces-of-work-family-conflict.

2. Rebecca Ray, Milla Sanes, and John Schmitt, "No-Vacation Nation Revisited," Center for Economic Policy Research, May 2013, http://cepr.net/publications/reports/no-vacation-nation-2013.

3. Alaska Oil Spill Commission, "Details About the Accident," *SPILL: The Wreck of the* Exxon Valdez, Final Report (reprint), State of Alaska, February 1990, accessed November 24, 2015, http://www.evostc.state.ak.us/index.cfm?FA=facts.details.

4. Marc Lallanilla, "Chernobyl: Facts About the Nuclear Disaster," LiveScience, September 25, 2013, http://www.livescience.com/39961-chernobyl.html.

5. Jennifer J. Deal, *Always On, Never Done? Don't Blame the Smartphone*, White Paper, Center for Creative Leadership, 2015, http://insights.ccl.org/wp-content/uploads/2015/04/AlwaysOn.pdf.

6. Jennifer Alsever, "Why This Startup Has a No-Workaholics Policy: Why One Company Punishes (Yes, Punishes) Staff Members for Not Taking Breaks," *Inc.*, February 2014, http://www.inc.com/magazine/201402/jennifer-alsever/no-workaholics-40-hour-week.html.

7. Duke Medicine News and Communications, "Sleep-Deprived People Make Risky Decisions Based on Too Much Optimism," *DukeMedicine*, accessed November 24, 2015, http://corporate.dukemedicine.org/news_and_publications/news_office/news/sleep-deprived-people-make-risky-decisions-based-on-too-much-optimism.

8. Claire Swedberg, "PantryLabs' Vending Machine Dispenses Fresh Foods via RFID," July 29, 2014, *RFID Journal,* http://www.rfidjournal.com/articles/view?12028.

9. "Nomophobia," *Wikipedia,* accessed February 4, 2016, https://en.wikipedia.org/wiki/Nomophobia.

10. Kostadin Kushlev and Elizabeth Dunn, "Checking Email Less Frequently Reduces Stress," *Computers in Human Behavior* 43 (2015): 220–228, https://www.academia.edu/9182785/Checking_Email_Less_Frequently_Reduces_Stress.

11. Molly Brown, "Nielsen Reports That the Average American Adult Spends 11 Hours Per Day on Gadgets," GeekWire, March 13, 2015, http://www.geekwire.com/2015/nielsen-reports-that-the-average-american-adult-spends-11-hours-per-day-on-gadgets.

12. American Academy of Pediatrics, "Media and Children," accessed December 4, 2015, https://www.aap.org/en-us/advocacy-and-policy/aap-health-initiatives/pages/media-and-children.aspx.

13. Shalini Misra et al., "The iPhone Effect: The Quality of In-Person Social Interactions in the Presence of Mobile Devices," *Environment and Behavior* (Impact Factor: 1.27), July 2014, doi:10.1177/0013916514539755.

14. William Powers, *Hamlet's BlackBerry: Building a Good Life in the Digital Age* (New York: Harper Perennial, 2011), 15.

References

Academy of Achievement. "John Wooden Interview." February 27, 1999. http://www.achievement.org/autodoc/page/woo0int-4.

Adobe. "State of Create: Global Benchmark Study on Attitudes and Beliefs about Creativity at Work, School and Home." April 2012. http://www.adobe.com/aboutadobe/pressroom/pdfs/Adobe _State_of_Create_Global_Benchmark_Study.pdf.

Alaska Oil Spill Commission. "Details About the Accident." *SPILL: The Wreck of the* Exxon Valdez, Final Report (reprint). State of Alaska. February 1990. http://www.evostc.state.ak.us/index.cfm ?FA=facts.details.

Alsever, Jennifer. "Why This Startup Has a No-Workaholics Policy: Why One Company Punishes (Yes, Punishes) Staff Members for Not Taking Breaks." *Inc.,* February 2014. http://www.inc.com/ magazine/201402/jennifer-alsever/no-workaholics-40-hour-week .html.

Amabile, Teresa, and Steven Kramer. *The Progress Principle: Using Small Wins to Ignite Joy, Engagement, and Creativity at Work.* Cambridge, MA: Harvard Business Review Press, 2011.

American Academy of Pediatrics. "Media and Children." Accessed December 4, 2015. https://www.aap.org/en-us/advocacy-and -policy/aap-health-initiatives/pages/media-and-children.aspx.

American Institute of Stress, The. "50 Common Signs and Symptoms of Stress." Accessed January 29, 2016. http://www.stress.org/stress-effects.

Arbor Day Foundation. "Elm." Accessed January 29, 2016. https://www.arborday.org/programs/nationaltree/elm.cfm.

Association for Psychological Science. "Take Notes by Hand for Better Long-Term Comprehension." Accessed February 4, 2016. http://www.psychologicalscience.org/index.php/news/releases/take-notes-by-hand-for-better-long-term-comprehension.html.

Austin, Michal. "Texting While Driving: How Dangerous Is It?" *Car and Driver*. June 2009. http://www.caranddriver.com/features/texting-while-driving-how-dangerous-is-it.

Bandura, Albert. "Self-efficacy." In *Encyclopedia of Human Behavior*, Vol. 4, edited by V. S. Ramachaudran, 71–81. New York: Academic Press, 1994. Reprinted in *Encyclopedia of Mental Health*, edited by H. Friedman. San Diego: Academic Press, 1998.

Bandura, Albert, and Nancy E. Adams. "Analysis of Self-Efficacy Theory of Behavioral Change?" *Cognitive Therapy and Research* 1 (1977): 287–310. doi:10.1016/0146-6402(78)90002-4.

Barnes, Brooks. "The Voice Behind Mick (and Others)." *New York Times*. June 7, 2013. http://www.nytimes.com/2013/06/09/movies/the-voice-behind-mick-and-others.html.

Baumeister, Roy F., Ellen Bratslavsky, Catrin Finkenauer, and Kathleen D. Vohs. "Bad Is Stronger Than Good." *Review of General Psychology* 5 (2001): 323–370. doi:10.1037//1089-2680.5.4.323.

Berkes, Howard. "30 Years After Explosion, Challenger Engineer Still Blames Himself." NPR. Updated January 29, 2016. http://www.npr.org/sections/thetwo-way/2016/01/28/464744781/30-years-after-disaster-challenger-engineer-still-blames-himself.

———"Remembering Roger Boisjoly: He Tried to Stop Shuttle Challenger Launch." Updated February 7, 2012. http://www.npr.org/

sections/thetwo-way/2012/02/06/146490064/remembering-roger-boisjoly-he-tried-to-stop-shuttle-challenger-launch.

Bernstein, Ethan S. "The Transparency Paradox: A Role for Privacy in Organizational Learning and Operational Control." *Administrative Science Quarterly* 57 (2012): 181–216. doi:10.1177/0001839212453028.

Brickman, Philip, Dan Coates, and Ronnie Janoff-Bulman. "Lottery Winners and Accident Victims: Is Happiness Relative?" *Journal of Personality and Social Psychology* 36 (1978): 917–927. doi:10.1037/00223514.36.8.917.

Bronson, Po, and Ashley Merryman. *NurtureShock: New Thinking About Children*. New York: Grand Central Publishing, 2009. Also available at https://books.google.com/books?id=AlknZbh bUPAC&pg=PT93&lpg=PT93&dq=study+writing+letters+of +gratitude+froh&source=bl&ots=2m7RCNOeEy&sig=7DzO 8i1dZvZkA0RnSqlav0fR4KA&hl=en&sa=X&ei=G-p8UteFKs fC4AOXzID4Cg#v=onepage&q=study%20writing%20letters %20of%20gratitude%20froh&f=false.

Brown, Molly. "Nielsen Reports That the Average American Adult Spends 11 Hours Per Day on Gadgets." GeekWire. March 13, 2015. http://www.geekwire.com/2015/nielsen-reports-that-the-average-american-adult-spends-11-hours-per-day-on-gadgets.

Buss, David M. "Human Mate Selection." *American Scientist* 73 (1985): 47–51. https://www.researchgate.net/profile/David _Buss/publication/233820651_Human_mate_selection/ links/00b7d52fe2ac5a9eed000000.pdf.

Callahan, Steven. *Adrift: Seventy-Six Days Lost at Sea*. New York: Mariner Books, 2002.

Caltech Counseling Center. "The Impostor Syndrome." Accessed January 19, 2016. https://counseling.caltech.edu/general/Infoand Resources/Impostor.

CancerConnect.com. "Laughter May Boost Immune System." Accessed November 25, 2015. http://news.cancerconnect.com/laughter-may-boost-immune-system.

Cant, Rona. *Snow, Sleds and Silence: The Story of the Nordkapp Expedition*. Faringdon, Oxfordshire: Libri Publishing, 2012.

Carney, Dana R., Amy J. C. Cuddy, and Andy J. Yap. "Power Posing: Brief Nonverbal Displays Affect Neuroendocrine Levels and Risk Tolerance." *Psychological Science* 21 (2010): 1363–1368. doi:10.1177/0956797610383437.

Centers for Disease Control and Prevention. "Healthcare-Associated Infections (HAI) Progress Report." Last updated March 3, 2015. http://www.cdc.gov/hai/progress-report.

Chambers, Richard, and Margie Ulbrick. *Mindful Relationships: Creating Genuine Connection with Ourselves and Others*. Wollombi, NSW, Australia: Exisle, forthcoming. Also available at https://books.google.com/books?id=IqZdCwAAQBAJ&pg=PP1&dq=ulbrick+mindful+relationships&hl=en&sa=X&ved=0ahUKEwj65p-65dzKAhUB-WMKHWtzBAIQ6AEIHTAA#v=onepage&q=ulbrick%20mindful%20relationships&f=false.

Cherry, Kendra. "The Asch Conformity Experiments." About Health. Updated May 17, 2015. http://psychology.about.com/od/classicpsychologystudies/p/conformity.htm.

Clarey, Christopher. "Olympians Use Imagery As Mental Training." *New York Times*, February 22, 2014. http://www.nytimes.com/2014/02/23/sports/olympics/olympians-use-imagery-as-mental-training.html?_r=0.

Conley, Mikaela. "Persistence Is Learned from Fathers, Says Study." ABC News. June 15, 2012. http://abcnews.go.com/Health/persistence-learned-fathers-study/story?id=16571927.

Cousins, Norman. *Anatomy of an Illness: As Perceived by the Patient*. New York: W.W. Norton & Company, 1979.

Coviello, Lorenzo, Yunkyu Sohn, Adam D. I. Kramer, Cameron Marlow, Massimo Franceschetti, Nicholas A. Christakis, and James H. Fowler. "Detecting Emotional Contagion in Massive Social Networks," *PLOS ONE*, March 12, 2014. doi:10.1371/journal.pone.0090315.

Coyle, Dan. "The Power of High-Leverage Practice." *The Talent Code* blog. Accessed November 24, 2015. http://thetalentcode.com/2014/11/24/the-power-of-high-leverage-practice.

Cross, Rob, Jane C. Linder, and Andrew Parker. *Charged Up: Managing the Energy That Drives Innovation.* The Network Roundtable at the University of Virginia. http://www.robcross.org/pdf/roundtable/energy_and_innovation.pdf.

Crum, Alia J., Peter Salovey, and Shawn Achor. "Rethinking Stress: The Role of Mindsets in Determining the Stress Response." *Journal of Personality and Social Psychology* 104 (2013): 716–33. doi:10.1037/a0031201.

Cuddy, Amy. "Your Body Language Shapes Who You Are." TED Talk. June 2012. http://www.ted.com/talks/amy_cuddy_your_body_language_shapes_who_you_are.

Dale Carnegie Training. *The 5 Essential People Skills: How to Assert Yourself, Listen to Others, and Resolve Conflicts.* New York: Touchstone, 2009.

Deal, Jennifer J. *Always On, Never Done? Don't Blame the Smartphone.* White Paper. Center for Creative Leadership. 2015. http://insights.ccl.org/wp-content/uploads/2015/04/AlwaysOn.pdf.

Del Giudice, Marguerite. "Grit Trumps Talent and IQ: A Story Every Parent (and Educator) Should Read." *National Geographic.* October 14, 2014. http://news.nationalgeographic.com/news/2014/10/141015-angela-duckworth-success-grit-psychology-self-control-science-nginnovators.

Derber, Charles. *The Pursuit of Attention: Power and Ego in Everyday Life*. Oxford: Oxford University Press, 2000.

Duckworth, A. L., C. Peterson, M. D. Matthews, and D. R. Kelly. "Grit: Perseverance and Passion for Long-term Goals." *Journal of Personality and Social Psychology* 9 (2007): 1087–1101.

Duke Medicine News and Communications. "Sleep-Deprived People Make Risky Decisions Based on Too Much Optimism." *DukeMedicine*. Accessed November 24, 2015. http://corporate.dukemedicine .org/news_and_publications/news_office/news/sleep-deprived -people-make-risky-decisions-based-on-too-much-optimism.

Durant, Will. *The Story of Philosophy: The Lives and Opinions of the World's Greatest Philosophers*. New York: Simon & Schuster/ Pocket Books, 1991 (originally published 1926).

Eblin, Scott. *Overworked and Overwhelmed: The Mindfulness Alternative*. Hoboken, NJ: Wiley, 2014.

Efferson, Charles, Rafael Lalive, Peter J. Richerson, Richard McElreath, and Mark Lubell. "Conformists and Mavericks: The Empirics of Frequency-Dependent Cultural Transmission." *Evolution and Human Behavior* 29 (2008): 56–64. http:// dx.doi.org/10.1016/j.evolhumbehav.2007.08.003.

Emmons, Robert. "How Gratitude Can Help You Through Hard Times." Greater Good. May 13, 2013. http://greatergood.berkeley .edu/article/item/how_gratitude_can_help_you_through _hard_times.

Ericsson, K. Anders, and Neil Charness. "Expert Performance: Its Structure and Acquisition." *American Psychologist* 49 (1994): 725–747. http://dx.doi.org/10.1037/0003-066X.49.8.725.

Eskreis-Winkler, Lauren, Elizabeth P. Shulman, Scott A. Beal, and Angela L. Duckworth. "The Grit Effect: Predicting Retention in the Military, the Workplace, School and Marriage." Frontiers in Psychology. February 3, 2014. doi:10.3389/fpsyg.2014.00036.

EY (Ernst & Young Global Limited). "Study Highlights: Work-Life Is Harder Worldwide." Accessed December 2, 2015. http://www.ey.com/US/en/About-us/Our-people-and-culture/EY-study-highlights-work-life-is-harder-worldwide#.Vl8BidKrR0u.

Fallon, Nicole. "Solving the Mystery of Gen Y Job Hoppers." *Business News Daily.* August 22, 2014. businessnewsdaily.com/7012-millennial-job-hopping.html.

Feiler, Bruce S. *The Secrets of Happy Families: Improve Your Mornings, Rethink Family Dinner, Fight Smarter, Go Out and Play, and Much More.* Kindle edition. New York: William Morrow, 2013.

Forest History Society, The. "Mann Gulch Fire, 1949." Accessed December 2, 2015. http://www.foresthistory.org/ASPNET/Policy/Fire/FamousFires/MannGulch.aspx.

Fox Cabane, Olivia. *The Charisma Myth: How Anyone Can Master the Art and Science of Personal Magnetism.* New York: Portfolio, 2013. Also available at https://books.google.com/books?id=WBVVgK0tYOkC&pg=PT29&lpg=PT29&dq=How+many+of+you+in+here+feel+that+you+are+the+one+mistake+that+the+admissions+committee+made&source=bl&ots=qit7HsujEF&sig=JUg72FHfeTWGT759Kr4AHBLctz0&hl=en&sa=X&ved=0ahUKEwia_rig29bKAhVN7mMKHcrADmoQ6AEIHTAA#v=onepage&q=How%20many%20of%20you%20in%20here%20feel%20that%20you%20are%20the%20one%20mistake%20that%20the%20admissions%20committee%20made&f=false.

Froh, Jeffrey J., and Giacomo Bono. "Gratitude in Adolescence: An Understudied Virtue." Available at https://docs.google.com/viewer?url=http://people.hofstra.edu/jeffrey_j_froh/spring%202010%20web/Gratitude%20in%20Adolescence%20Encyclopedia%20Entry_sent%20to%20Roger_R1_12.29.09.pdf.

Frost, Nicole, Lyndsay Nickolai, Sheyla Desir, and Roseanne Fairchild. "From Our Readers: How Mentorship Affects Retention Rates of New Nurses." *American Nurse Today* 8 (2013). http://www.americannursetoday.com/from-our-readers-how -mentorship-affects-retention-rates-of-new-nurses.

Gachman, Dina. "Stephen King: His Ten Best Quotes on Writing." SSN. October 16, 2013. http://www.ssninsider.com/stephen -king-his-ten-best-quotes-on-writing.

GCC Insights. "Stress—The Hidden Threat in Every Workplace." *GCC Blog.* Posted March 5, 2015. https://www.gettheworld moving.com/blog/stress-insights-report.

Generation Grit. "Time to Practice What We Preach." July 3, 2014. http://www.generationgrit.com/blog3/2014/7/2/time-to -practice-what-we-preach.

Gilbert, Daniel. *Stumbling on Happiness.* New York: Vintage, 2007.

Gonzales, Laurence. *Deep Survival: Who Lives, Who Dies, and Why.* New York: W. W. Norton & Company, 2003.

Grant, Adam. "Finding the Hidden Value in Your Network." *HuffPost Business.* Updated August 18, 2013. http://www .huffingtonpost.com\adam-grant\finding-the-hidden-value -_1_b_3458536.html.

Gruenert, Steve, and Todd Whitaker. *School Culture Rewired: How to Define, Assess, and Transform It.* Alexandria, VA: ASCD, 2015.

Guenzi, Paolo, and Dino Ruta. *Leading Teams: Tools and Techniques for Successful Team Leadership from the Sports World.* Hoboken, NJ: Jossey-Bass, 2013.

Guest, Phyllis. "The Growing Problem of Workplace Bullying." November 17, 2011. Workplace Bullying Institute. http://www .workplacebullying.org/guest.

Hackman, J. Richard. "Leading Teams: Setting the Stage for Great Performances—The Five Keys to Successful Teams." Harvard Business School Working Knowledge. July 15, 2002. http://hbswk.hbs.edu/archive/2996.html.

Haddad, Marie Reine. "Impostor Syndrome: No You Are Not a Fraud." The NICHD Collection. Eunice Kennedy Shriver National Institute of Child Health and Human Development. April 2, 2014. https://science.nichd.nih.gov/confluence/display/newsletter/2014/04/02/Impostor+Syndrome%3A+No+You+Are+Not+a+Fraud.

Hale, Laura. "Generation Grit: Retro-Inspired Action Figures." Kickstarter. Accessed December 3, 2015. https://www.kickstarter.com/projects/1882390019/generation-grit.

Hamori, Monika, Jie Cao, and Burak Koyuncu. "Why Top Young Managers Are in a Nonstop Job Hunt." *Harvard Business Review*, July–August 2012. https://hbr.org/2012/07/why-top-young-managers-are-in-a-nonstop-job-hunt/ar/1.

Harvard Business Review. Harvard Business Review on Collaborating Effectively. Jackson, TN: Perseus Books Group, 2011.

Harvard Business Review. "Mindfulness in the Age of Complexity." March 2014. https://hbr.org/2014/03/mindfulness-in-the-age-of-complexity.

Hassan, Fred. *Reinvent: A Leader's Playbook for Serial Success.* New York: Jossey-Bass, 2013. Also available at https://books.google.com/books?id=6ywwofiaw18C&pg=PT130&lpg=PT130&dq=fred+hassan+If+you+are+in+a+position+of+making+a+sale+and+doing+something+you+are+not+comfortable+with%E2%80%94something+you+won%27t+feel+proud+of+later&source=bl&ots=U_nNCx0Hp2&sig=OnVFceU8E3Gm4sHSd-F37zg4mcE&hl=en&sa=X&ved=0ahUKEwi39v7t0JDKAhVH8j4KHSO0C5YQ6AEIHTAA#v=onepage&q=if%20you%20are%20in%20a%20position&f=false.

Hawkley, Louise C., Ronald A. Thisted, Christopher M. Masi, and John T. Cacioppo. "Loneliness Predicts Increased Blood Pressure: Five-Year Cross-Lagged Analyses in Middle-Aged and Older Adults." *Psychology and Aging* 25 (2010): 132–141. doi:10.1037/a0017805.

Holacracy. "How It Works." Accessed January 29, 2016. http://www.holacracy.org/how-it-works.

Hotten, Russell. "Volkswagen: The Scandal Explained." BBC News. December 11, 2015. http://www.bbc.com/news/business-34324772.

Kahneman, Daniel. *Thinking Fast and Slow.* New York: Farrar, Straus and Giroux, 2011.

Kantor, Jodi, and David Streitfeld. "Inside Amazon: Wrestling Big Ideas in a Bruising Workplace." *New York Times.* August 15, 2015. http://www.nytimes.com/2015/08/16/technology/inside-amazon-wrestling-big-ideas-in-a-bruising-workplace.html.

Keppel, Bruce. "Pacific Bell Calls Halt to Disputed Training Plan." *Los Angeles Times.* October 30, 1987. http://articles.latimes.com/1987-10-30/business/fi-11672_1_pacific-bell.

Kinjerski, Val, and Berna J. Skrypnek. "Creating Organizational Conditions That Foster Employee Spirit at Work." *Leadership & Organization Development Journal* 27 (2006): 280–295. doi:10.1108/01437730610666037.

Klopp, Hap. *Conquering the North Face: An Adventure in Leadership.* Bloomington, IN: iUniverse, 2012.

Kushlev, Kostadin, and Elizabeth Dunn. "Checking Email Less Frequently Reduces Stress." *Computers in Human Behavior* 43 (2015): 220–228. https://www.academia.edu/9182785/Checking_Email_Less_Frequently_Reduces_Stress.

Lallanilla, Marc. "Chernobyl: Facts About the Nuclear Disaster." LiveScience. September 25, 2013. http://www.livescience.com/39961-chernobyl.html.

Liker, Jeffrey. *The Toyota Way: 14 Management Principles from the World's Greatest Manufacturer.* New York: McGraw Hill Professional, 2003.

Litchfield, Robert C., Cameron M. Ford, and Richard J. Gentry. "Linking Individual Creativity to Organizational Innovation." *The Journal of Creative Behavior* 49 (2015): 279–294, doi:10.1002/jocb.65.

Lynch, Kevin. "Record Holder Profile: Juliana Buhring—Fastest Circumnavigation by Bicycle." Guinness World Records. November 6, 2013. http://www.guinnessworldrecords.com/news/2013/11/record-holder-profile-juliana-buhring-%E2%80%93-fastest-circumnavigation-by-bicycle-52724.

Macnamara, Brooke N., David Z. Hambrick, and Frederick L. Oswald. "Deliberate Practice and Performance in Music, Games, Sports, Education, and Professions: A Meta-Analysis." *Psychological Science* 25 (2014): 1608–1618. doi:10.1177/0956797614535810.

Maestripieri, Dario. "What Monkeys Can Teach Us About Human Behavior: From Facts to Fiction." *Psychology Today.* Posted March 20, 2012. https://www.psychologytoday.com/blog/games-primates-play/201203/what-monkeys-can-teach-us-about-human-behavior-facts-fiction.

Martin Luther King Jr. and the Global Freedom Struggle. "The Three Dimensions of a Complete Life." Accessed February 1, 2016. http://kingencyclopedia.stanford.edu/encyclopedia/documentsentry/doc_the_three_dimensions_of_a_complete_life.

McGonigal, Kelly. "How to Make Stress Your Friend." TEDGlobal 2013. TED Talk. June 2013. http://www.ted.com/talks/kelly_mcgonigal_how_to_make_stress_your_friend?language=en&utm_source=Shawn%27s+Blog+Updates&utm_campaign=0657f5a034-RSS_campaign&utm_medium=email&utm_term=0_76214e7fb1-0657f5a034-33416069.

"Meghan Vogel, Ohio Track Star, Carries Runner Across Finish Line at State Competition." YouTube video, 0:45. Posted by "New Everyday News!" August 24, 2012. https://www.youtube.com/watch?v=H1F9hRFUr6I.

Merck KGaA Darmstadt. *State of Curiosity.* Executive Overview. September 9, 2015. http://www.125yearssmartertogether.com/wp-content/uploads/2015/09/1509_Merck_Executive-Summary_R8a1.pdf.

Michigan State University. "Abusive Leadership Infects Entire Team." *ScienceDaily.* August 20, 2014. http://www.sciencedaily.com/releases/2014/08/140820091703.htm.

Milmo, Cahal. "Has a Cure Been Found for Dutch Elm Disease?" *The Independent.* June 7, 2010. http://www.independent.co.uk/environment/nature/has-a-cure-been-found-for-dutch-elm-disease-1994102.html.

Misra, Shalini, Lulu Cheng, Jamie Genevie, and Miao Yuan. "The iPhone Effect: The Quality of In-Person Social Interactions in the Presence of Mobile Devices." *Environment and Behavior* (Impact Factor: 1.27). July 2014. doi:10.1177/0013916514539755.

Monster. "Dangerously Stressful Work Environments Force Workers to Seek New Employment." Accessed December 1, 2015. http://www.monster.com/about/a/Dangerously-Stressful-Work-Environments-Force-Workers-to-Seek-New-Empl4162014-D3126696.

Moser, Jason S., Hans S. Schroder, Carrie Heeter, Tim P. Moran, and Yu-Hao Lee. "Mind Your Errors: Evidence for a Neural Mechanism Linking Growth Mind-Set to Adaptive Posterror Adjustments." *Psychological Science* 22 (2011): 1484. Originally published online October 31, 2011. doi:10.1177/0956797611419520.

Mueller, Claudia M., and Carol S. Dweck. "Praise for Intelligence Can Undermine Children's Motivation and Performance."

Journal of Personality and Social Psychology 75 (1998): 33–52. http://dx.doi.org/10.1037/0022-3514.75.1.33.

Muraven, Mark. "Building Self-Control Strength: Practicing Self-Control Leads to Improved Self-Control Performance." *Journal of Experimental Social Psychology* 46 (2010): 465–468. doi:10.1016/j .jesp.2009.12.011.

Newheisera, Anna-Kaisa, and Manuela Barretoa. "Hidden Costs of Hiding Stigma: Ironic Interpersonal Consequences of Concealing a Stigmatized Identity in Social Interactions." *Journal of Experimental Social Psychology* 52 (2014): 58–70. doi:10.1016/j .jesp.2014.01.002.

Newsweek. "John Wooden: First, How to Put on Your Socks." October 24, 1999. http://www.newsweek.com/john-wooden-first-how -put-your-socks-167942.

NFL. "Odell Beckham Makes Catch of the Year!" YouTube video, 1:15. Posted January 25, 2015. https://www.youtube.com/ watch?v=zxbz3DDQzHU.

Nicolson, Harold. *Dwight Morrow.* New York: Harcourt, Brace and Company, 1935.

Nyberg, Anna, Lars Alfredsson, Tores Theorell, Hugo Westerlund, Jussi Vahtera, and Mika Kivimä. "Managerial Leadership and Ischaemic Heart Disease among Employees: The Swedish WOLF Study." *Occupational and Environmental Medicine* 66 (2009). 51–55. doi:10.1136/oem.2008.039362.

O'Conner, Patricia T., and Stewart Kellerman. "Out of Pocket, Revisited." *Grammarphobia Blog.* April 16, 2010. http://www.gram-marphobia.com/blog/2010/04/out-of-pocket-revisited.html.

Ophira, Eyal, Clifford Nass, and Anthony D. Wagner. "Cognitive Control in Media Multitaskers." *Proceedings of the National Academy of Sciences,* 106 (2009): 15583–15587. doi:10.1073/ pnas.0903620106.

Ormrod, Jeanne Ellis. *Educational Psychology: Developing Learners*, 5th ed. Upper Saddle River, NJ: Pearson/Merrill Prentice Hall, 2006.

Ozcelik, Hakan, and Sigal Barsade. "Work Loneliness and Employee Performance." *Academy of Management Proceedings,* January 2011 (Meeting Abstract Supplement): 1–6. doi:10.5465/AMBPP.2011.65869714.

Padilla-Walker, Laura M., Randal D. Day, William Justin Dyer, and Brent C. Black. " 'Keep On Keeping On, Even When It's Hard!': Predictors and Outcomes of Adolescent Persistence." *The Journal of Early Adolescence* 33 (2013): 433–457 (first published on June 18, 2012). doi:10.1177/0272431612449387.

Parker, Lyndsey. "Judith Hill on Jamming with Prince, Remembering Michael Jackson, and What 'The Voice' Taught Her About America." Yahoo Music. October 21, 2015. https://www.yahoo.com/music/s/judith-hill-on-jamming-with-prince-remembering-004526004.html.

Pascale, Richard, Jerry Sternin, and Monique Sternin. *The Power of Positive Deviance: How Unlikely Innovators Solve the World's Toughest Problems.* Cambridge, MA: Harvard Business Review Press, 2010.

Patrick Smith's Ask the Pilot. "The Heroics of Captain Sully and the 'Miracle on the Hudson.'" Accessed January 30, 2016. http://www.askthepilot.com/questionanswers/sully-and-heroics.

Pennebaker, James W. *Opening Up: The Healing Power of Expressing Emotions.* New York: The Guilford Press, 1997.

Phys.org. "Study Reveals That Many People Are Oblivious to How They Come Across to Counterparts, Colleagues." June 30, 2014. http://phys.org/news/2014-06-reveals-people-oblivious-counterparts-colleagues.html.

Piff, Paul. "Does Money Make You Mean?" TED Talk. October 2013. https://www.ted.com/talks/paul_piff_does_money_make_you_mean?language=en.

Pinker, Susan. *The Sexual Paradox: Men, Women and the Real Gender Gap.* New York: Scribner, 2009.

Powers, William. *Hamlet's BlackBerry: Building a Good Life in the Digital Age.* New York: Harper Perennial, 2011.

Ray, Rebecca, Milla Sanes, and John Schmitt. "No-Vacation Nation Revisited." Center for Economic Policy Research. May 2013. http://cepr.net/publications/reports/no-vacation-nation-2013.

Reeve, Christopher. *Nothing Is Impossible: Reflections on a New Life.* New York: Ballantine Books, 2004.

Ridley, Matt. "When Ideas Have Sex." TED Talk. July 2010. http://www.ted.com/talks/matt_ridley_when_ideas_have_sex.

Rockoff, Jonah E. *Does Mentoring Reduce Turnover and Improve Skills of New Employees? Evidence from Teachers in New York City.* Working Paper 13868. NBER Working Paper Series. National Bureau of Economic Research. March 2008, 33. doi:10.3386/w13868.

Rudolph, Jenny W., and J. Bradley Morrison. *Confidence, Error, and Ingenuity in Diagnostic Problem Solving: Clarifying the Role of Exploration and Exploitation.* Draft Version 1. Winter 2007. http://people.brandeis.edu/~bmorriso/documents/Confidence ErrorIngenuityinDx.pdf.

Schaffer, Grayson. "The Toughest Woman on Two Wheels." *Outside.* April 29, 2015. http://www.outsideonline.com/1970876/toughest-woman-two-wheels.

Seligman, Martin E. P. *Authentic Happiness: Using the New Positive Psychology to Realize Your Potential for Lasting Fulfillment.* New York: Free Press, 2002.

——— *The Optimistic Child: A Proven Program to Safeguard Children Against Depression and Build Lifelong Resilience.* New York: Houghton Mifflin, 1995.

Senay, Ibrahim, Dolores Albarracín, and Kenji Noguchi. "Motivating Goal-Directed Behavior Through Introspective Self-Talk: The

Role of the Interrogative Form of Simple Future Tense." *Psychological Science* 21 (2010), 499–504. doi:10.1177/0956797610364751.

Shannonhouse, Rebecca. "Is Your Boss Making You Sick?" *Washington Post*. October 20, 2014. https://www.washingtonpost.com/national/health-science/is-your-boss-making-you-sick/2014/10/20/60cd5d44-2953-11e4-8593-da634b334390_story.html.

Siebert, Al, Kristin Pintarich, and Molly Siebert. *The Survivor Personality: Why Some People Are Stronger, Smarter, and More Skillful at Handling Life's Difficulties—And How You Can Be, Too.* New York: Perigee, 2010. Also available at https://books.google.com/books?id=8n5YAuG2xB4C&pg=PT136&dq=The+best+survivors+spend+almost+no+time,+especially+in+emergencies,+getting+upset+about+what+has+been+lost,+or+feeling+distressed+about+things&hl=en&sa=X&ved=0ahUKEwih_puEqMDJAhXMQCYKHQU6CKwQ6AEIIzAB#v=onepage&q=The%20best%20survivors%20spend%20almost%20no%20time%2C%20especially%20in%20emergencies%2C%20getting%20upset%20about%20what%20has%20been%20lost%2C%20or%20feeling%20distressed%20about%20things&f=false.

Simpson, Joe. *Touching the Void*: *The True Story of One Man's Survival*. New York: HarperCollins Publishers, 1988.

Singhal, Arvind, and Karen Greiner (abridged version prepared by Prucia Buscell). "Do What You Can, with What You Have, Where You Are: A Quest to Eliminate MRSA at the VA Pittsburgh Healthcare System." Plexus Institute. *Deeper Learning* 1 (2007). http://c.ymcdn.com/sites/www.plexusinstitute.org/resource/collection/6528ed29-9907-4bc7-8d00-8dc907679fed/VAPHS_PD_MRSA_Story_Condensed_-_Final.pdf.

Smith, James Pat. "Leadership and Mission in Resilient Organizations: Hancock Bank As a Case Study." Community and Regional Resilience Institute. Accessed January 12, 2016. http://www.resil

ientus.org/wp-content/uploads/2013/03/GP_Resilience_Essay
_Hancock_Bank_Final_8409_1249429792.pdf.

Spreitzer, Gretchen, and Christine Porath. "Creating Sustainable
Performance." *Harvard Business Review*. January–February 2012.
https://hbr.org/2012/01/creating-sustainable-performance.

Sutton, Bob. "Bob Sutton: Power Poisoning." YouTube video, 1:51.
Posted by "Stanford eCorner." Uploaded November 23, 2010.
https://www.youtube.com/watch?v=TDBWg9e_cZk.

Sutton, Robert. "Is Your Future Boss a Demeaning Creep?" Bloomberg
Business. June 23, 2015. http://www.businessweek.com/business
_at_work/bad_bosses/archives/2008/06/is_your_future.html.

Swartz, Luke. *Overwhelmed by Technology: How Did User Interface
Failures on Board the USS* Vincennes *Lead to 290 Dead?* 2001.
http://xenon.stanford.edu/~lswartz/vincennes.pdf.

Swedberg, Claire. "PantryLabs' Vending Machine Dispenses Fresh
Foods via RFID." *RFID Journal*. July 29, 2014. http://www.rfid
journal.com/articles/view?12028.

Taylor, Lynn. "Bad Boss Behaviors Rise Up to 50%; Says Five-
Year Comparative Study." PR Newswire. October 7, 2009.
http://www.prnewswire.com/news-releases/bad-boss
-behaviors-rise-up-to-50-says-five-year-comparative-
study-63685702.html.

Thompson, Ben. "Joe S. Simpson." Bad Ass of the Week. Accessed
November 29, 2015. http://www.badassoftheweek.com/simp
son.html.

Tvspots.tv. "AIG—Laughing Baby Ethan." Posted March 3, 2011.
http://www.tvspots.tv/video/52586/aig-laughing-baby-ethan.

University of Michigan's Ross School of Business. "Understanding
the Impact of Positive Deviance in Work Organizations." July 4,
2004. https://michiganross.umich.edu/rtia-articles/understanding
-impact-positive-deviance-work-organizations.

U.S. Forest Service. "1910 Fires: Edward Pulaski." Accessed December 2, 2015. http://www.fs.usda.gov/detail/r1/learning/history -culture/?cid=stelprdb5122876.

Vaughan, Diane. *The Challenger Launch Decision: Risky Technology, Culture, and Deviance at NASA.* Chicago: University of Chicago Press, 1997.

Ware, Bronnie. *The Top Five Regrets of the Dying: A Life Transformed by the Dearly Departing.* Carlsbad, CA: Hay House, 2012.

Warneken, Felix, and Michael Tomasello. "The Roots of Human Altruism." *British Journal of Psychology* 100 (2009): 455–471. doi:10.1348/000712608X379061.

Weihenmayer, Erik. *The Adversity Advantage: Turning Everyday Struggles into Everyday Greatness.* New York: Touchstone, 2007.

Wikipedia. "Chuck Taylor (salesman)." Accessed January 29, 2016. https://en.wikipedia.org/wiki/Chuck_Taylor_(salesman).

———. "Dutch Elm Disease." Accessed January 15, 2016. https:// en.wikipedia.org/wiki/Dutch_elm_disease.

———."Nomophobia." Accessed February 4, 2016. https:// en.wikipedia.org/wiki/Nomophobia.

Wildland Fire Leadership Development Program. "Staff Ride to the South Canyon Fire." Accessed December 2, 2015. http://www .fireleadership.gov/toolbox/staffride/library_staff_ride9.html.

Williams, Joan C., and Heather Boushey. *The Three Faces of Work-Family Conflict: The Poor, the Professionals, and the Missing Middle.* Center for American Progress. January 25, 2010. https:// www.americanprogress.org/issues/labor/report/2010/01/25/7194/ the-three-faces-of-work-family-conflict.

Winner, David. "ESPN FC: Beautiful Game. Beautiful Mind." ESPN. May 16, 2012. http://espn.go.com/IndexPages/news/ story?id=7938409.

Wiseman, Richard. *The Luck Factor.* Santa Monica, CA: Miramax, 2003.

Yoshino, Kenji, and Christie Smith. *Uncovering Talent: A New Model for Inclusion.* Deloitte University Leadership Center for Inclusion. Updated December 6, 2013. https://www2.deloitte .com/content/dam/Deloitte/us/Documents/about-deloitte/us -inclusion-uncovering-talent-paper.pdf.

Young, Valerie. *The Secret Thoughts of Successful Women: Why Capable People Suffer from the Impostor Syndrome and How to Thrive in Spite of It.* New York: Crown Business, 2011.

Zijlstra, Fred R. H., Mary J. Waller, and Sybil I. Phillips. "Setting the Tone: Early Interaction Patterns in Swift Starting Teams As a Predictor of Effectiveness." *European Journal of Work and Organizational Psychology* 21 (2012). doi:10.1080/13594 32X.2012.690399.

Index

About the Author

Shawn Hunter is an entrepreneur, best-selling author, and currently founder and president of Mindscaling, a company creating beautiful, intelligent online learning courses based on the works of best-selling authors. Learn more at mindscaling.com

Shawn is an accomplished speaker. He delivers dynamic, practical, entertaining, and "high content" presentations to audiences around the world. Learn more at shawnhunter.com

Until July 2015 Shawn was executive producer and vice president for leadership solutions at Skillsoft. For more than decade, Shawn has interviewed, collaborated with, and filmed hundreds of leading business authors, executives, and business school faculty.

Shawn originally cofounded Targeted Learning Corporation with his father, Hal Hunter, PhD, which was acquired by Skillsoft in February 2007.